yes is a world

JAMES W. ANGELL

WORD BOOKS, Publisher • Waco, Texas

D1625487

Contents

Introduction

One of the top-ranked songs of the early seventies was a light-hearted thing called "Welcome to My World."

All human encounters which are warm and cordial mean that. And this book is a welcome into the world of yes—into the life of affirmation.

Life cannot be ignored.

If it is not affirmed, it is denied.

If it flounders endlessly in the seas of directionless doubt, it is denied.

If it is wasted by hating, coveting, or killing, it is denied.

If it is forfeited "day by dragging day in a thousand small, uncaring ways," it is denied.

If its liberties are not extended equally to both sexes, and all races, it is denied.

But when life is celebrated, tasted, lived, spent, painted, danced, shared, and set to music—all under the banner of some innate, imperishable yes—then, it is affirmed.

The sun shines.

Our own personal history is redeemed from absurdity.

1. Yes is a world

Under every No
Lies a passion for Yes that has never been broken.

Wallace Stevens

The other day I drove to a nearby shopping center and came home with a book.

It wasn't planned that way, but we often go shopping and return with the unexpected. Like Father takes the car in for a brake job and comes home with a brand new model. Or Mother stumbles onto a clearance sale at the Show-Off. In she strides, hours later, striped boxes piled higher than her head.

I didn't get my "book" at a bookstore, however. Nor off one of those rotating display racks at a supermarket checkout stand.

I didn't even pay for it.

11

Yes is a world

I found it in a clothing shop window. A gray houndstooth-patterned suit was on display there, plus an oyster shirt, and a red silk tie. Underneath: a pair of shiny black Florsheims —$39.95. And the book.

It was fourteen words long. A quotation by e. e. cummings. Printed on a small, white card in flowing script and inserted as an attention-grabber, it read:

> "yes is a world
> & in this world of
> yes live
> (skilfully curled)
> all worlds" [1]

What follows is meant to be an expansion of that single, singing sentence and philosophy which has been ricocheting around in my head ever since I first saw it at the Plaza. Like a handball driven lightning hard against some court-wall of the mind it comes blazing its way back daily into my routine, and I must duck, or find a way to send the ball back into play.

"Yes" is the finest word in our language, and we must learn to pronounce it.

In an age of ambivalence where not only suits are gray, but also our religion and ethical decisions, the sound of Yes needs to be heard, the world of Yes identified as the most important of all the frontiers of the human heart.

To say that life is Yes is not to cast a vote for an anti-intellectual, we-know-it-all kind of fundamentalism. It is not to deny that life is filled with crazy dilemmas and irrational happenings which seem to contradict the idea that *anyone* around here is in charge. It is to say, however, with confidence, that God has let a few small rays of light leak through the crack of the Mysterious Door, and that he is busy in our world—even in the midst of disappointment and heartache. That's enough to make Yes a stronger word than No.

Is the universe some deliberate artwork of God? **Yes.**

Does God know we are here, and is his love a Love which outlasts and outlives our own? **Yes.**

Is there hope for me—after I have failed? Can I say Yes to myself as a person, even when my performance wasn't what it should have been? **Yes.**

Is it right for us to dream the Impossible Dream—to go on attempting to reach the Unreachable Star? **Yes.**

After life is there More? **Yes.**

Honestly? **Yes.**

For Yes is a world—an optional world—but definitely a world. The most splendid, enduring world of all. And, in that world, dwell all the others.

If Yes is life's gladdest word, which wins the prize for being the saddest? Cancer? Death? Divorce?

Oscar Hammerstein, who gave us *Oklahoma* and *South Pacific*, came up with a surprising selection. The saddest word in the whole language, he said, is "but."

"You have many outstanding qualities, *but* . . ."

"I am in favor of this, *but* . . ."

"I was going to write to you, *but* . . ."

"I know that you are my brother, *but* I must kill you because of the international situation."

In a parable Jesus once told concerning some people who begged off a banquet invitation, the list of regrets ran something like this:

"I have bought a field. I must go look at it."

"I just purchased five cows. I need to go and try them out to see if they're good work animals."

"I got married yesterday. You'll have to wait till I get back from my honeymoon."

Translated into 1974, such alibis sound only slightly changed:

"I'm sorry, *but* I'm broke."

"I'm sorry, *but* I'm busy."

"It's for a good cause, *but* I still owe for taxes!"

Without excuses we would lose our sanity within days. Because we can't do everything. We can't support everything. We can't *like* everything without winding up counterfeit human beings. We must make choices. If No has a melancholy sound, it may also add up to the price of poise and personal effectiveness.

We can't answer every telephone, solve every problem, die on every cross.

But, in Jesus' story, the invitation is *God's*. It includes the invitation to enjoy him, break bread with him, trust him. *This* invitation is special.

The thesis of this book is that we can find ways to respond to God and live all of life with an eagerness and ecstasy similar to the kind Joyce wrote about when he described the powerful attraction of physical love:

> And then I asked him with my eyes to ask again yes
> And then he asked me would I yes
> And first I put my arms around him yes
> And drew him down to me so he could feel
>   my breath and perfume yes
> And his heart was going like mad
> And yes I said yes I will yes.[2]

Yes, life has meaning.

It is not a farce, not a "tale told by idiots, signifying nothing."

And, yes, you are *accepted*, says the Christian faith. You will not be kept cooling your heels out in some crummy waiting room adorned with last year's copies of *Good House-keeping* while God makes up his mind as to your right to enter his Kingdom. You are welcomed in.

Saying Yes to ourselves at the same time the world may be treating our presence disinterestedly is easier said than done, but it *can* be done.

This conversation is reported to have taken place one weekday night in a family living room: "I'm not going back to school tomorrow, and I'll give you three reasons why. The first is: the teachers don't like me; the second is: the kids don't like me; and the third is: even the people in the cafeteria don't like me."

This reply followed: "You *are* going back to school tomorrow, and I'll give you three reasons why. The first is: you are six feet tall; the second is: you are fifty years old; and the third reason is: you are the *principal!*"

There are days when many of us feel like saying: "I'm not going back to life tomorrow!" There are, though, always opposite, compelling reasons that tell us why we should and which explain why we will.

For one thing, we are tremendously important to each other's happiness and that is bound to make us important to God.

A teacher wrote in the margin of a theme my previously discouraged son had submitted as part of an English assignment: "I see the beginning of eloquence." Part of the assignment all of us have as human beings is to go about saying that to each other, exposing that truth *within* each other.

Of Jesus the New Testament says: "All God's promises find their Yes in him." He is, for many of us, the Scout on the trail, the welcoming Host of Bright Angel Lodge. And the future is not a frightening blank. Instead it is alive with hope and powerful possibilities. Yes, rather than No.

In one of Rod Serling's TV programs there was a man who unexpectedly found himself able to see accurately and precisely into the future. Since he *knew* what the stock market would do ahead of time, and which horses would win which races, he found it easy to become rich. He knew what the weather would be, so he could plan confidently for those activities where it was a factor. He knew which political parties would prevail; that meant other important personal advantages. All this seemed good to him. He could even read the newspapers of the future, before events themselves happened. Then, one day, in the process of boning up on things to come, he stumbled onto his obituary.

It is part of the favor of God that we cannot see ahead. We can see yesterday, and, with God's help, we can accept whatever tomorrow brings. That's enough.

While the shape or nature of the future's frontier will vary, we never give up our role as frontiersmen. The "front" at times, seems to vanish. Then it dons a new theatrical costume and reappears on stage.

Marriage and sexuality—institutions which once may have seemed firmly settled—have become a frontier. The right to die. The right to live. The ethics of leisure. Planetary survival.

In my lifetime, space has seemed to be the most dramatic new frontier of the century. John F. Kennedy called it the "new ocean." And Arthur Clarke wrote, after the first moon landing: "The doors of heaven are opening."

Another frontier, far from being exhausted, is inward space. The fact that the moon has turned out to be so dark, cold, and presumably dead has perhaps intensified our search

16

to strike a balance between the world without and the world within. Faith has always walked a tightrope between these two, and it has demonstrated that it possesses a self-righting capacity whenever one set of interests attempts to overpower the other.

The inward journey presently is in the ascendancy in religious thought, and this may be right. We will have more to say about life's transcendent moments later, because they are part of the formula of Yes—but no more so than the Yes which pulses through the tortuous outward journey toward justice and true social community.

In his "Prayer for the Seventies," Norman Corwin compares today's technological showmanship to our inability to pass the simple tests of interhuman acceptance. Addressing God, he says:

> Your antique miracles have been trumped by solemn science:
> Daily the patent office registers intenser magic than the burning bush:
> The serpent from the rod becomes a ruby laser;
> The leper is healed by mycins;
> The blind draw vision from an eye bank.

> That, being the case, dear busy God, please manifest thyself again through one superlative, new-minted covenant:

> Create for the lot of us—all nations indivisible—an Act of God more stupendous than mere parting waters or a standing sun
> A miracle harder to come by that would, if consummated, cause dry bones from all the hundred holocausts to meet and dance,
> And charter stars to sing together in the brightest chancel of imponderable space.

17

And this is what the miracle would be:
That man should love his kind in all his skins and pig-
ments

And kill no more.

Repeat that we should love our kind
And kill no more.
Yes, granted such a miracle is asking very much of you.

But it is long past time to ask.

God, do your thing.[3]

The natural world with its goldfinches, blue skies, green forests, white snows, children's laughter and Sunday afternoon walks also adds up to some great multicolored YES hung out across the sky like heavenly laundry.

Sometimes we press and strain so hard trying to get ahead in the world of material achievements we grow old without knowing we are passing—daily—through a magnificent arboretum. Finally, with all bases covered, and ready for retirement, we may realize we have existed in only one dimension, have never learned one of the most important of all the arts of living: hearing life's Yes music along the way— and making sure that our love is paid up as well as our life insurance.

One July day a Bible salesman was working the territory of a lower middle-class neighborhood in a small midwestern town. He was poorly dressed, and the engine of his old Studebaker rattled as he drove up and down the elm-lined street. Anyway, it was a living, even during the depression.

No one had much money. But the Word of God—well, that was something else. What it had to say, what it had the power to mean in people's lives and dreams was above the criterion of what one could or could not afford.

The summer special was a large study Bible bound in

flexible black leather. In addition to the Scriptures, it also contained a concordance, articles about the Holy Land, and maps. The price was $30. As an extra come-on, and, for a limited time only, the buyer would also receive, for the one price, a copy of Hurlbut's *Stories of the Bible*.

To make the offer absolutely irresistible the purchase could be handled on an installment basis: $3 a month for ten months, with $1 extra as a "carrying charge."

My mother signed up.

Now, twenty-five years into the ordained ministry, that scene comes back to me. Are our lives little deliberate schemes of God?

As we look forward to what may come—to what the future holds for each one of us, we probably must say that, if there is a Plan, it is hidden in the heart of God. We have to operate, live, choose, and attempt to "be" as if no preordained arrangement exists. To act otherwise would be to unfairly limit our humanity and responsibility.

The freedom to shape and manage the future according to our most far-out dreams is the essence of the Christian Spirit. God has not preempted the unknown but has told us to enter the new country of Tomorrow unafraid.

In Harbor City, California, four-year-old Robert Craig whispered to his mother, "Mom, Daddy doesn't have any arms or legs, does he?"

"No, he doesn't," Sally Craig replied.

"Let's not tell him," said Robby.

Noble Craig, the father, who lost both legs and his right arm to a booby trap in Vietnam, instructed that word of his injuries go first to his father. The elder Craig was thus able to tell Sally before the telegram came. Sally says she knows how wives of returning POWs feel when they meet their husbands.

"It's hard. You practice and practice what you're going

19

to say when you first see him, but when that moment comes
. . . there's nothing there in your throat to come out," she
says.

"When I made that long walk down the corridor to see
Noble for the first time, my knees were shaking. It was the
longest walk of my life. But I couldn't let him down."

"Don't worry, honey. Everything is going to be all right,"
Craig said, with a fractured jaw and wired teeth. He had also
lost his hearing and the sight in his right eye.

Today he laughs. He goes to woodwork classes. He hunts
with his father, swims, raises tropical fish, and has taken up
motorcycle riding.

"I can't drive," he says, "but I can sure hang on to some-
body who is driving!"

Under every No lies some Yes which cannot be broken. We
may not be able to drive a motorcycle because we have no
legs, but we can hang onto a vision.

Jesus is the Yes that God has endorsed across the face of
the world. Written in the tender language of one brief span
of years, and mirrored from *that* life into our own, Jesus
becomes a better explanation of Reality than anything else
we have. And our faith-relationship with him generates in us
the ability to convert much of our despair into new oppor-
tunity.

Robert Raines expresses it most wonderfully for everyone:

> Lord, we are uneasy looking into the future
> we need to know that you are with us
> and we are with you
> Give us the confidence that though all things change
> You are the same God
>   ever gracious
>   from whose love nothing can separate us
> Let us feel you on our pulses

and in our breathing
and convince us in our very bodies
that we live and die
in the hollow of your hand
Release now those mute longings
   hidden in our hearts
to join the early morning birdsong
singing green beginnings
and multicolored hopes
   for you are shaking us and
   shaping us into
   a springtime people
   with Easter in our eyes.[4]

Or should we spell that *"ayes"*?

2. Man is born with rainbows
in his heart

*The rainbows of one good utopian are worth
more than the mud puddles of a thousand cynics.*

Dr. Roderic Gorney

It's strange how some days wind up all No while other days
everything is Yes.

We talk about "getting out on the wrong side of the bed."
Or shrug: "This just *isn't* my day!" The washing machine
starts to growl, then grinds to a halt. The kids wake up with
sore throats. The mail is late. The freeway traffic is a dis-
aster. The weather is rotten. The world is a mess.

But those *other* days! Days when the pieces of our lives fit
together with jigsaw perfection, when we feel like sauntering
down the violet-bordered walkways of life, singing "There's a
rainbow 'round my shoulder, and the sky is blue above . . . ."

Rainbows from the beginning have been understood as a
huge Yes sign in the sky.

22

In a gradually clearing sky Noah and his skeleton crew see a rainbow, which they take to be a sign that the world is ready for a fresh start.

The storm of chastening is over. And God can be counted upon never again to lay waste the earth.

The sun shines.

The bow glimmers.

In the distance there are soft flutelike sounds, and in the place of thunder, lightning, and driving water, all that remains is a new chance.

In our scientific way of examining the environment we now know what kinds of physical phenomena produce rainbows. We've broken light up into its different wave lengths. We understand trigonometry, refraction, ultraviolet wave lengths. We've measured light's speed. But all this doesn't prevent us from enjoying the story of flood and the rainbow, or from understanding it as one of the vehicles of the truth that God is trustable and that he cares about each one of us.

The Church is a rainbow community. And when the Church *lives* as hope's honest illustration, the world will once again take it seriously.

It is hard to figure out where we are in the mid-seventies. The Indo-China war has almost disappeared from the morning headlines, but we have been terribly battered and bruised by the agony it produced. Our hearts are still recuperating. We're still not sure we've "got our heads on straight." What we plan to do, or what kind of new world we hope to build now that this sad sequence is mostly behind us, may be too early to say. The Watergate scandal has produced more disillusion. Working in the Church is being compared to rearranging deck chairs on the *Titanic.* No particular songs seem to be on people's lips. It's not an age of despair. It's more like a nameless time, without enthusiasm, and, except for ecology, without many great objectives or passions. History seems to be pausing. A new world is coming, but the train is late.

What can thoughtful people hope for in the 1970s and '80s? And what can hope be tied to?

There's a line by Carl Sandburg that exactly fits our need. For me, it's enough to lift my heart out of the dumps any day of the year.

Wrote America's favorite minstrel, "Man is born with rainbows in his heart, and you'll never read him unless you consider rainbows." [1]

Old demons give plenty of evidence they are still about. People still trample each other. They despise and kill. They hate, and do a hundred things which seem to suggest that man is a beast, a selfish, cruel, lustful, foul-mouthed blemish on the face of an otherwise beautiful planet.

In Autumn 1972, I wrote:

> The whole world is Munich.
> All men are Jews.
> Civilization is weeping
> In barracks 31.
>
> Bicycles racing;
> Runners gaining;
> Vaulters vaulting;
> Discuses spinning;
> Swim waters thrashing;
> Volleyball players spiking;
> Wrestlers straining;
> Gold medals shining;
>
> But the jungle winning. [2]

We can't refute such changes convincingly.

And Jesus did not deny them, either. His preaching rather

seemed modeled after the gut-level accusations of the Baptist. Jesus is often pictured in our minds as a patient, loving shepherd, seeking out the lost and lame. But Jesus was also a man of steel, an offender as well as a defender. He did not minimize human failure. Neither, though, did he give up on his belief that we are simultaneously the fond children of the Father's heart—lamps in which burns some kind of holy flame.

A woman I know said she had to go to the bus station recently to meet a friend who was arriving at 4:30 A.M. "That's one way," she said, "to get another slant on the human situation—to be around a bus station two hours before dawn."

A girl is raped and stabbed and left to die on a Santa Monica beach. She had come West, from Chicago, just five months before.

The 38-year-old head of a family of four children is cut down by leukemia at the moment he is needed most.

Hale Boggs, trying to help out an aspiring young candidate for office, loses his life as a result of some mechanical failure in an airplane, or a quirk of weather.

A soldier stands trial for "fragging"—a word-dividend of Vietnam, which means deliberately killing one's own kinsman in a spirit of revenge or dislike.

The drug traffic continues, reaching ugly fingers down into our elementary schools. The waiting list for people to undergo methadone treatment runs into the thousands.

And we sing, and write tracts on hope?

Yes, because for every item which suggests that life's social fabric is rotten, that all we need is a little more time before we totally destroy ourselves by pollution and war, there is a parallel item on the positive side of the Ledger of Man.

Doctors heal, and families pray.

25

Yes is a world

Boys and girls learn and dream.

René Dubos, a man of outstanding achievements in the field of microbiology, lives in the Hudson Valley above New York City. He writes with optimism about the irrepressibility of a mysterious force he calls "the God Within":

> The exuberance of nature in the spring appears almost indifferent to dangers. Undaunted by lawn mowers, dandelions return cheerfully every year, even on the most carefully tended lawn. Unconcerned with automobile traffic, woodchucks and rabbits graze along superhighways. Years ago, peregrine falcons used to forsake the cliffs of the New Jersey Palisades for the ledges of New York skyscrapers. And over Jamaica Bay immense flocks of birds take off not far from the flight patterns of jet aircraft over Kennedy airport.
>
> Despite the suffering, despair, and ugliness created by racial conflicts, national rivalries, food shortages, and pollution, the bells of Easter always lift me on waves of hope. To experience a spring day is enough to assure me that eventually life will triumph over death. On bomb craters in the midst of cities after the Second World War delectable wild mushrooms appeared, as if to symbolize that life will continue to generate order and beauty from physical decay. Men have known for thousands of years that the phoenix can be reborn from its ashes. Our form of civilization may be sick and dying, but through the desolate, wintry climate of our times, there is beginning to emerge an effervescence of expectancy . . .[3]

When we live in hope, we help hope to happen. Hope is in faith's blood. But hope must be redefined by every newly arriving generation, perhaps by each newly arriving person who cries his way onto the scene—who comes to share with the rest of us the exhilarating drama of Being.

Said Zophar to Job:

"You will forget your misery;
you will remember it as waters
that have passed away.
And your life will be brighter
than the noonday;
its darkness will be like the morning.
And you will have confidence
because there is hope;
you will be protected
and take your rest in safety.
You will lie down
and none will make you afraid."

(Job 11:16–19, rsv)

I hope for a better world—for my children and grand-children and those who will come after them. I hope for a cleaner world, a fairer world with less racial isolation, a cancerless world, a schizophrenialess, bombless world.

But I hope even more I will not miss love and persons, wonder and value while I am waiting for that more authentic, more intended world to gasp and fight its way into existence.

Some hope is apocalyptic in nature and there's a place for that, too.

The "return" of Jesus is a puzzle for most people. But there's one way in which it is not a puzzle—by the manner in which it says: don't look for God's presence completely in the past. Look for him in the life of Now. Jesus did not come in the first place in the way most seers had predicted. And he may not come in the way this generation expects. That's okay. What is not okay—what is tragic, and what hope fiercely resists—is that men will live expecting nothing. Nothing except death, or some automated Tomorrowland

27

which, we realize in our most honest moments, has no more power in itself to produce happiness than the one that is already here.

Hope is not simply the vision of a future paradise.

It is also the centering in of our confidence in God in a way which liberates us from worry, tension, and an eternal paralysis of analysis. It is the art of learning to rest our anxieties in the love and the adequacy of God. The future is too big for us to pile up on our own mental doorsteps. We can't ignore it and say it's not ours to fashion. Neither can we let it smother our joy and enthusiasm for the immediate moment.

James Thurber said, "Let us not look forward in fear, nor backward in regret, but around us in awareness."

And Thomas Merton wrote: "Hope empties our hands, so we *can work with them.*"

Lift your glass, then, to hope! To hope, updated for our own explosive generation and translated into behavior which results in our at least trying to build God's world in the images of Yes.

. One caution: hope can be dangerous if we allow it to become a substitute for action. But it has all the *pow!* of nuclear fission if we understand it as God's respiration—breathing courage through us into his half-defeated creation.

Is there a rainbow in your life, in mine? Yes. The God who both cries in a manger in Bethlehem and dies on a cross in Jerusalem can still tell us who we are. He can remind us that nothing can separate us from God's sovereign friendship.

The Bible begins with a story about a rainbow, and closes with one, too. In the Revelation there's a description of an angel from heaven who appears "wrapped in a cloud, with a rainbow over his head, his face like the sun, and his legs like pillars of fire."

28

Maybe God just likes bands of bright color.

That's a crazy guess.

But it's something other than guessing to say our lives have magic meanings which faith can help us discover. That's an announcement that has come to us engraved on angel wings.

3. Tears, laughs, loves, and thrills

There's a touchstone that I always apply to a book before I publish it, and, believe it or not, it came from William Randolph Hearst. It was a commercial note that hung above Joe Connally's desk at King Features, and it said, "Tears, Laughs, Loves, and Thrills." That was the rule for everybody writing for the American Weekly. *They had to have all those things in their stories in equal amounts. And when I first started, I realized that Shakespeare and everybody else who ever wrote successfully had all of those things. Of course, if I kept that in the front of my mind, I'd never get anywhere. But when I check over a manuscript, it always comes to my mind.*

Ted Giesel

Tears, laughs, loves, and thrills.

The four corners of the human heart. At some point in our history our lives touch all four bases. Each spells Yes in its own noninterchangeable.way.

Ted Giesel, who, as Dr. Seuss, gave us such fantastic children's books as *The Cat in the Hat* and *To Think That I Saw It on Mulberry Street*, talked about this emotional quartet in a newspaper interview. The sign above Joe Connally's desk, mentioned in the headnote, was meant, he said, to help writers write with sharp, human authority. If tears, laughs, loves, and thrills were all included in the writer's story, readers would be bound to read it, because everyone would be able to say: "That's *me*: I've been there!"

God meets us on all four levels.

We experience him when we stare into the rich, red depths of the Grand Canyon or lie on our backs on a summer night and look up at the constellation Orion, sensing in its subtle movement the slow steady spin of the earth. We encounter God in Bach, Beethoven and Brahms. We encounter him in our back yard ablaze with hibiscus, chrysanthemums, and phlox. Christianity says we meet God in history, too, with unique clarity focused in the Man of Nazareth.

But let's start where Ted Giesel starts—with tears. That's one with an early beginning.

A young girl whom I had never seen before ran up to our front door one day and pushed the bell. Her eyes were electric with fear, and her mouth was ringed in perspiration. She looked about fourteen—half woman, half little girl. But she was all child as she poured out to me, a total stranger, her dilemma. Three other girls had chased her, she said, and threatened to beat her because of a wisecrack she had made at a recent football game. They were from another neighborhood, but had tracked her down. They were closing in, and she was terrified.

But tears at age fourteen aren't our first by any means.

Tears begin—even before we've opened our eyes to see in what sort of world we've landed—and we never lose our need to let them fall. In most cases they represent wholesome release, and we do not need to feel ashamed of them.

They are part of the price of being persons.

When we are called upon to endure great sorrow, we need to be told that grief is the partner of love. If we love deeply, we must hurt deeply, too. One is the cost of the other.

God probably has his own need for tears, too—perhaps occasioned by regret that he overestimated man's capacity to use his freedom in constructive rather than destructive ways.

Tears seem bound up with that one poignant word everyone understands: help!

Character actor Van Heflin, whose death was reported in the newspapers not long ago, was described by his friends as being "a very lonely man." A plush Hollywood hotel as a home address wasn't much help for that. Loneliness is a form of woundedness.

Judith Schwab talks about loneliness in her poem "Man at the Counter":

> Sucking warm coffee
>   from his morning cup,
> He sits and listens, holding
>   a napkin to his knee.
>
> His eyes search the faces
>   that come new and different
> But he speaks to no one,
>   goes through the cigaret paces.
>
> Silent yet, he folds his lips
>   around the smoke, then
> Slowly blows the air,
>   hunches up his back and sips.
>
> Some of his best thoughts he sees
>   daring, dreaming, warm
> In this disguised ritual
>   of straight and thick security.[1]

In a growth group, the leader looked across a circle and saw a young woman in whom all of life's beauty and sparkle seemed to have disappeared. Cutting right to the heart of her problem, he asked, sympathetically, "Who ran over you?"

When Tony Conigliaro quit the California Angels baseball team, he announced his decision at a 5:00 A.M. press conference. Just before boarding a plane back to New York, he commented to a reporter concerning the team's management: "They don't know you're hurting unless they see the bone sticking out."

Or tears may represent the damp conclusion that we have failed at something:

> In my own life I kept coming apart..
> Half the things I tried
> Never left the runway. I
> Was moral as could be.
> But, at the cross, I heard *you* cry.
>
> Your dream exploded. And, as the heart-rain fell
> Across my face, I clutched my raincoat
> And made the sign of peace.
>
> —James W. Angell

Joy, it has been suggested, is the happiness we feel when we have faced adversity and survived.

Laughter is next. It's the medicine of the spirit—the impromptu song we sing to keep life from breaking us in two.

A world without comedy would be like nature without giraffes or parrots, clothes without silver buttons. We need to laugh at life and trouble. When we laugh at ourselves we have the towers of internal freedom in view. We need to laugh about growing old, about politics, about our sexuality, and even about death.

The day following my mother's death, two cousins (who were like brothers to me) came from Colorado to Iowa to attend the funeral service and show their concern. Frank and John and I had grown up together and gotten into all the usual kinds of teenage trouble. Not having seen each other for years, we quickly fell to discussing old times, for, when death comes, the past surges in like a Pacific tidal wave. Talking late into the night, we found ourselves rolling on the floor with nostalgic joy, reliving those delicious small-town, small-boy years. I remember thinking, is this right? Here I am in the midst of the greatest loss I have known and I'm laughing like a fool! About then I caught a glimpse of my mother's face. She was nodding her approval of all this raucous behavior. Nothing could please her more than to see the three of us doing what we were doing.

Laughter is the oxygen of courage, the noisy evidence that the full weight of the world does not belong to us, and that we are not stuck with the responsibility of being our own saviors.

And *love.*

Teilhard de Chardin wrote: "Some day—after mastering the winds, the waves, the tide, and the gravity—we shall harness for God the energies of love and then, for the second time in history of the world, man will have discovered fire."

St. John defined it:

". . . Love is of God, and he who loves is born of God . . . for God *is* love" (1 John 4:7,8).

If it is easier to find tears in the Bible than side-splitting one-liners, it is also the easiest kind of job we could give ourselves to find references to love.

Isaac and Rebecca.

David and Jonathan.

Ruth and Naomi.

Ruth and Boaz.

Jesus and Lazarus.

Or Paul: "Love knows no limit to its endurance, no end to its trust, no fading of its hope; it can outlast anything. It is, in fact, the one thing that still stands when all else has fallen" (1 Cor. 13:7-8, Phillips).

To love is to own everything. Not to love is to be stuck with only shadows of the truth.

Human love is the code which we use to decipher what divine love is all about, and, as a minister, I rarely pass a Sunday by without trying to make that point.

If we intend to hold the interest of our readers, says Dr. Seuss, love has to be one of our stops!

At a going-away, thank-you party, Frances, a family friend, entertained some dinner guests with a couple of songs, accompanying herself on an autoharp. She said temperature changes in the room could mean the harp would sound a bit out of tune. But she added: "Actually, there's only one string on my harp anyway, and that's love."

To love well we need to anchor our love in the love of God for us. That love is the purifier and direction-finder for all our efforts to love on the level of persons.

Further, we cannot have a great nation without love— love between neighbors, and between the diverse elements of our huge, multifaceted society. We may have a big country. Lots of cash. Lots of factories. Lots of guns. But no great country unless we love.

There, then, is the carousel and ferris wheel. And clowns, doing pratfalls and making their noses light up. Love, laughter, and tears over the rain that fell, almost spoiling the performance. But we've still one thing to do—one set of feelings still left to experience whether Hearst's advice is right: ride the roller coaster!

How could we describe Creation itself without talking about "thrills"? Beauty, yes. Wonder, okay. Amazement, reverence—certainly. But also thrill—ecstatic, body-tingling, mind-boggling pizzazz!

"Thrills" could suggest to our imagination those skydivers or acrobats we saw at the county fair, the big race, that memorable game for the Superbowl trophy. But consider, too, those first Seven Days of fashion designing. Or Moses and Pharaoh. And what about Samson yanking down the temple walls with unbelievable strength, or Palm Sunday's parade! But now an early morning stillness is interrupted by a sound. Not a birdsong. Not a cart rumbling by. Not a bell tolling across the Kidron, nor a donkey celebrating the return of light. But a voice—man's voice, uttering one, short, familiar word: "Mary!"

Yes's finest hour!

Webster suggests synonyms for "thrill": "vibrate," "shiver," "tremble," or "throb." The Resurrection is all four, and then some.

It's interesting to ponder what kind of human experiences do these wild, wonderful things to us. We all have our lists. They might be short, but we each have one—C-major moments, when our universes shudder or explode like Krakatoa in 1833. When something inside us shatters our complacency and wonderlessness into a billion shards. As if we suddenly knew that Someone had inserted an angel inside of us and it was more than we could contain.

Tears. Laughs. Loves. Thrills.

They make up the yellows, greens, scarlets, and blues of the event-process we call "being." They are the universal experiences which at times threaten to consume us, but wind up making us strong, gentle, dependent upon each other, and upon the God from out of whose love all life proceeds.

Fused, they help us glorify the dust out of which we were made and fit us for a larger life which never ends.

4. Not the postponed life

*God is the poet of the world, with tender patience
leading it by his vision of truth, beauty, and
goodness.*

Alfred North Whitehead

Ernest Gordon, Dean of the Chapel at Princeton University, tells how after Christmas Eve service on the campus one year, a rather shabbily dressed man made his way through the crowd of worshipers and thrust a small paper sack into his hand. In it was a book of poems, and two or three other possessions of such nature it was obvious they were the most cherished things he owned.

But it was Christmas. Students were shouting greetings to the chaplain. He was trying to return their holiday wishes, and in the press of people and the general excitement of the happy night, the man who had brought the bag of gifts vanished, unidentified.

Two weeks later, Dr. Gordon says, he picked up the morning paper and saw the man's picture on an inside page. He had been struck and killed while walking along a highway.

Two ships had passed on the night of shepherds. A hurried hailing—a short exchange of flashing-light signals. But before any actual communication had had a chance to take place, the possibility had vanished. Time rushed forward toward her next surprise.

Some things in life deserve not to be postponed. Other things must be. We can't do everything worth doing.

Choices, we have to make.

Inevitably we wind up with a certain residue of regret: Why didn't I do that? I forgot it! I put off writing that note. I shouldn't have!

Lady Bird Johnson, after the death of her husband, Lyndon, spoke about having two memory lists which she calls "Aren't you glad thats," and "If onlys—." She said she found peace in the realization that the first was longer than the second.

One of the ways faith helps us minimize regret is by keeping pressure on us to choose the important over the unimportant. Each day is an ice-cream cone, melting in the heat of the clock. Each minute is a ballet, existing for a minisecond—no more. A day isn't like a painting we can hang on a wall or a piece of music we are able to play back again twenty-four hours later. Whenever we utter the word "today," we are acrobats perched on one hand, feet thrust into the air, from a flagpole atop the Sears tower in Chicago (that's the highest in the United States now!). When we say "today" we are looking at a flash of sun, seeing the fast flutter of some bluebird wings, saying a word that is half hello, half good-by.

Michel Quoist says in one of his prayers about time: "God, I know I have time to do everything you want me to do."

38

That's good to keep in mind whenever we think about the things that seem to us so awfully urgent. In giving to others, it may help to remind ourselves that God never asks us for what we do not have. It's when we *have* and don't share that we have a basis for believing we are in trouble with him.

God isn't present in our lives to drive us goofy with unreasonable expectations. Instead, he is present to keep us from making the *wrong* kinds of demands upon ourselves and to keep us from emptying our lives down velvet ratholes.

When we speak about what we ought *not* to postpone, we also ought to speak about things which deserve to *be* postponed—like worry, frustration, the thought of "getting even." Jealousy and slander also should be dropped from the curriculum.

Each day needs to be lived to the full—for the sake of that day, not as a day lived as preparation for another to come.

Theodore Roethke wrote: "Don't sit on the secret of life so long you forget it's there."

And look out for:

"Tomorrow I will be twenty-one; *then* I will start to live."

"Tomorrow we can be married; then we will be happy."

"Tomorrow the house gets paid for. Then all our financial anxieties will be over."

"Tomorrow the children will be grown and out on their own. Then I'll be free to think only about myself."

"Tomorrow I'm going to retire, then there'll be nothing left to do except to enjoy life."

Tomorrow can be a dangerous word!

It's a beautiful word, too, because life would be impossible without plans. But it's a burdensome word if we are depressed, if Wednesday seems sure to be just like Tuesday!

Tomorrow is as glad, or as sad, a word as we are willing to make it.

However we might feel about counterculture values and thinking, some important forms of social learning have been going on during the past ten or fifteen years. Regardless of how many good things we can point to about the American system, it is still true that that system has tended to produce people who are often so success-conscious they wind up as the major shareholders of "the postponed life."

There is never time to live today because one is always getting ready for tomorrow. Work. Sacrifice. Room at the top. Keep up. Improve your situation. Be prepared. Look ahead. Family reputation. Security. Status.

For some this has meant no time to play, no time to think, no time for children, no time to stop and examine a flower, or to listen to the thoughts of an eleven-year-old boy.

Suppose for the next two years you were to be given the guarantee of exemption from worry about money or any other related responsibilities, set free to do anything you wanted to do. Your only motivation: the pure satisfaction of exploiting your own aliveness.

What would you do? Travel? Paint? Write? Climb mountains? Enter a university? Go to some deprived part of the world to see what you could do to make life better there? What choice would you make?

Because of a "Protestant ethic" upbringing, many of us have tended to see leisure only as intermittent reward. We are frontier stock, and that means: Clear the land. Build that road. Make a million dollars. Then maybe some day we can go to Palm Springs or Palm Beach and play golf every day of the week.

I'm glad I was born with some of this desire to achieve, to wring each day dry. But I don't want such values to preempt all others. I don't want to wind up stuck with the postponed life—a life which is 75 percent anticipation and 25 percent realization.

Another way to avoid postponed living is to become convinced that every situation, every human season has within it the raw material of greatness. God has made everything useful and good "in his time."

Even tragedy is a crucible for selfhood, and suffering can always be "turned inside out."

Wrote the German poet Rainer Maria Rilke:

How should we be able to forget those ancient myths about dragons that at the last minute turn into princesses who are only waiting to see us once beautiful and brave. . . . Perhaps everything terrible is in its deepest being something helpless that wants our help.[1]

It's easy to come to the point where we tune out help cries very easily. We can develop cocoons around ourselves, find nineteen reasons not to respond. "I didn't want to get involved." "Help!" can become as lifeless a word as "love" in a pornographic film.

But if we are sometimes disappointed by other persons in their behavior, and if we disappoint ourselves because we know we are not what we ought to be, our hopes still soar when, in some unplanned-for emergency, human beings work together, spare no cost, toss self-interest totally aside to save a life, purchase a kidney machine, or save a trapped coal miner.

God helps people *through people*. Each of us has a gift God can use. And when we say Yes to someone else's plea for our involvement, we enter with them into the brave world of meaning.

James, the brother of Jesus, wrote: "You are a mist that appears for a little time, then vanishes."

Celebrate, then, the temporary! Catch a falling star. Life is a polka-dotted butterfly. Like manna in the wilderness,

41

life won't keep. It must be eaten day by day, celebrated hour by hour.

The New Testament challenges us to lay up for ourselves "treasures in heaven," and no single lesson of life seems to take us longer to learn. Here's a check list. This week:

Mend a quarrel.
Seek out a forgotten friend.
Dismiss suspicion and replace it with trust.

Write a love letter. Share a treasure.
Give a soft answer. Encourage youth.
Manifest your loyalty in word and deed.
Keep a promise. Find the time.

Forego a grudge.
Forgive an enemy. Listen.
Apologize, if you were wrong.
Try to understand. Flout envy.

Examine your demands on others.
Think first of someone else.
Appreciate. Be kind; be gentle.
Laugh a little.
Laugh a little more.

Take up arms against malice.
Deserve confidence. Decry complacency.

Express your gratitude. Go to church.
Welcome a stranger.
Gladden the heart of a child.

Take pleasure in the beauty
and the wonder of the earth.

Speak your love.
Speak it again . . . .
Speak it still once again.

"Life is a celebration!" [2]

5. Champagne out of a tin cup

In the midst of flashing neon darkness,
We dare this day to celebrate the light.
In the midst of blaring, shouting silence,
We dare this day to celebrate the word.
In the midst of bloated, gorged starvation,
We dare this day to celebrate the bread.
In the midst of bottled, bubbling thirst,
We dare this day to celebrate the water.
In the midst of smothered, gnawing doubt,
We dare to celebrate the affirmation.
In the midst of frantic, laughing death,
We dare this day to celebrate life,
—with trembling.
Sing alleluia—rejoice!

I remember as a boy peering long and interestedly one night through a three-dimensional viewer at a picture of the tipped tower of Pisa. It was even more fun than television.

When I grew to manhood I had a chance to see the tower for real. In 1965 my wife, three of our children and I took the overnight express from Rome to Paris, a trip that included a ten-minute stop at Pisa.

I recall two things about our fifteen-minute stay. One, how we craned our necks to see if we could glimpse the leaning monument from the window as the train coasted into town. We did, through the red-amber light of a six o'clock sun.

Second, buying box suppers through an open train window

as we paused in the station wrapped in shadows. Fried chicken, rolls, salads, clay pots of beans, and bottles of warm, sweet wine.

Wine, for Europeans, is what coffee and tea are to Americans—the cosmopolitan drink. The tending of vineyards in Italy and the Rhineland is the livelihood of millions. In Europe, wine is called *vino*, the fruit of the vine.

The story of Jesus' changing of water into wine at a wedding at Cana, which appears only in John, is the frontispiece of the Gospel. John bases his account on seven key incidents in the life of Jesus. He calls them "signs" and sees them as translucent actions which demonstrate that God is offering our world a key to the house of Yes.

One is the healing of a blind man. John tells that story, then discusses his Lord as "the Light of the World." He describes the feeding of the five thousand solid reason for calling Jesus the Bread of Life. When an appreciative woman pours her costliest possession over the feet of Jesus, this is preface to a soliloquy on death and burial.

In the wine-and-wedding miracle, life is stated in festival terms, a concept not meant to be canceled by the cross. Jesus, whose spirit is full of sand and salt, talk and trees, and who does his teaching from a boat as a gentle March rain descends upon the loosely assembled crowd, helps us recognize the difference between a mere physical aliveness and a larger aliveness of which we are capable but not always conscious.

A group of young people took over the leadership of a worship service one morning and startled their parents by lifting their arms and shouting exultantly: "Come Alive!" Later, a member of the congregation likened the swinging hour which followed to "champagne out of a tin cup."

The Rolling Stones, a rock group, performed at the Los

Angeles Forum. The second of two performances to an SRO crowd began at 1:30 A.M. and ended five hours later.

Compared to the fun of skiing at Sun Valley, animated conversations over cocktails, intense excitement over who will win the Academy Awards, or professional football, the Church often seems dead, rigid, and inhibited.

If the Church allows itself to become just one more prison, then taps it is. Instead, it ought to be a set of moments when we become most expansively, openly, and honestly ourselves.

Yet it is in the Church where we often find it hardest to be ourselves; where we are often the most guarded, the most paranoid, the most unsure of being accepted and understood.

The Church, though, we ought to be quick to add, has no monopoly on human disguises or phoniness. What it has uniquely is a message which informs us that we can be free with God, and that God can set us free from ourselves.

Addictive drugs represent the attempt to achieve freedom from pain—even the pain of being forced to go on living. But there is no freedom in drugs. Drugs lead into the most dead-end street ever built.

To be *awake* is to be in pain.

Don't laugh. It's true. To be awake is to be in a state of low-keyed pain, so constant and natural we don't even notice it. To be *awake* means things are coming at us which demand our *at-tension*.

Freedom's roots are in faith, hope, and love—not in a bottle, a needle or a pill.

When we are ill and fight back against disease, our bodies call upon the regiments of Life. When we struggle against lethargy of soul our Spirit does the same thing.

To be alive is also to be aware of other people, other sufferings and yearnings.

Touching generates awareness. To touch a child's face, a

dog's smooth coat, a petaled flower, the rough surface of a rock, is to set up new orders of brain motion. To touch is to communicate. It is to possess. To own.

Freedom and aliveness also rise up as the fragrant incense of our decisions. To love is to exercise an option. We may try to avoid commitment because we want to keep some running room, but if we avoid it forever, we turn into slaves. To be alive is to leap into the sea. It is to pit our arms against the resistance of history and time. It is to shout our own special version of Yes against the midnight quiet of the town.

For the Church to be alive, it must develop new resilience, the capacity to pick itself up off the canvas and fight again. It must learn how not to overvalue its successes (as it did in the fifties), and, equally, not to become trapped or discouraged by its famine years (the sixties).

It's been great to hear the sound of steel bands invading stagnant sanctuaries. But this would be dull, too, if this were all we were to hear week after week. We don't need to shoot out the stained glass windows because their traditional character lacks some novelistic glamor. We don't leave home because we discover gulfs between generations. And we don't have to insult the past in order to be hospitable to the future. What we do have to do is to be *open* to all the fresh impulses of God's spirit, and to covet an attitude of adventure.

And aliveness is action.

"Life," as Peter Marshall expressed it, "is not duration, but donation." Perhaps we need to be done with so much TV-style, secondhand experience. To sing rather than being sung to. Create excitement for living by our own life-plunge, rather than trying to buy it in cellophane.

The truth lying in wait for us in the story of the changing of water into wine is that faith results in the sacramental conversion of *all* things. Every day comes to have its own way of dazzling us. A walk up a hillside turns out to be not a disgusting inconvenience, but a rendezvous with God; a rainstorm, a damp splendor rather than a reason to complain.

Is this what you are saying: "Sorry, but life isn't that way. Sure, there are moments of exhilaration and romance, days when life is carnival and jubilee. But most living is bread, not cake. Routine and duty. Getting the work out, and going to the dentist."

But we don't have to settle for anyone else's narrow summary.

The call to the champagne life is the call to the constant rediscovery of beauty, meaning, and people.

It doesn't mean things will always go well, or that God wants us to sit and grin while we listen to a recitation of yesterday's Belfast casualties, or hear of devastating floods which have wrecked the lives of other children of God. We are not asked to be deaf or blind; only poised between trouble and triumph. We are called to live each day as if it mattered —to believe that each human relationship we are party to, matters.

We are invited to live in the confidence that our lives are irreplaceable and indispensable. Jesus *has* come, and because of him Life is possible. Not empty, not a Clifford Irving hoax.

It is the high Sierras; it is daring a million things.

Engraved in my pulpit are the words: "Sir, we would see Jesus." Each time I walk into that holy box, I ask God to help me to help people see Jesus not as plastic prop for religion, but as the Man for others who can show all of us what to do with our humanity—how we can make it resonate and shine.

A bar in San Francisco is called "The Glass Crutch." We all have crutches, though not all of them are glass. We try to fill our lives with something to fight off despair or to make the future look interesting. We buy the latest fad in clothes; we

47

go to the theatre. We follow the political wars, our favorite team; read our horoscopes.

These may not all be crutches, but neither do they suffice for the thirsty cisterns of the soul.

We approach God from all points of the compass of human need. All are represented in most typical gatherings—our need for love, for forgiveness, for a way to conquer irrational fears, for help in making decisions we know will have far-reaching consequences; the need to get close to others or to have Someone in our lives to say thank you to because favorable things have happened to us; the need to be healed of a debilitating illness. In the Yes of Bethlehem lies an answer for these needs and the promise of God's mighty support.

Clara Byers died June 20, 1973, a few months past her ninetieth birthday. Forty-nine years before, in a village called Kachek, on the South China island of Hainan, her young missionary husband had been shot by bandits near his home, leaving her with four young children, another soon to be born. As George Byers lay on the ground, dying from bullet wounds in his stomach (Bob, the eleven-year-old son had run to the compound for help), he said: "Clara, I don't know what you're going to do, but Christ will take care of you." If there is anything Clara was quietly sure about through all these years, it is that Christ did.

Perhaps you don't like champagne. But the taste for life itself—there's where none of us can say that we do not care.

And God says: go ahead—get drunk on wonder. Drink long and deep from life's tin, but overflowing, cup!

6. You can listen to silence

*"You can listen to silence, Reuven. I've begun to
realize that you can listen to silence and learn
from it. It has a quality and a dimension all its
own. It talks to me sometimes. I feel myself alive
in it. It talks. And I can hear it."*

cA fourth-grade teacher who wanted to give her children
an exercise in creativity asked them to complete a sentence
beginning "Let's be as quiet as . . ." From answers compiled
by that teacher, Constance Fauci, and printed in the *New
York Times* in 1962, Michael Colgrass, a young composer,
developed a rare piece of symphonic music.

"Let's be as quiet," says the composition, as:

—A Leaf Turning Colors
—An Uninhabited Creek
—An Ant Walking
—Children Sleeping

Yes is a world

—Time Passing
—A Soft Rainfall
—The First Star Coming Out

If you want to have fun with your mind, try adding to his list.

Though I couldn't express it as exquisitely as the children, I thought about soundless gliders soaring, clouds changing position, a Quaker praying.

There are two kinds of silence. Both are part of the life of Yes.

First, the beautiful silences: the creatively healing, enjoyable silences which help us keep our sanity and go back to life restored after having lost a battle or two.

In Isaiah (30:15) there is this phrase: "In quietness and in trust shall be your strength." Silence is often able to put back what the hard engagements of living have subtracted from us.

There's the magic silence of Christmas Eve.

The soft, hundred-year-old feeling we feel when we stand, for the first time, inside the Lincoln Memorial and gaze up at a man who would have understood our times well, because his own were even grimmer.

The silence of mountains . . .

> I have an understanding with the hills
> At evening when the slanted radiance fills
> Their hollows, and the great winds let them be,
> And they are quiet and look down at me.
> Oh, then I see the patience in their eyes
> Out of the centuries that made them wise.[1]

50

And the morning! Those first hours seasoned souls learn to call the best:

> I met God in the morning
> when the day was it its best
> And his presence came like sunrise,
> like a glory in my breast.[2]

The benediction of a deserted church, especially when the afternoon sun soothingly washes its inner walls with dabs of reflected color.

Or the quiet that prevails between two people who love each other and do not need words, do not trust words to express all the radical things they feel about their love. Silence often does a better job than language.

So God comes to us silently and still, as if we were walking with a loved one upon a night of darkness, the air still save for the distant hum of the great city, and no sound save the fall of our footsteps. No word is spoken for no word is needed. Thus does God speak to a man in silence and answer his prayers out of the great echoing unknown. Thus does a man brood upon God with no embarrassment if he can find no true word to express his thoughts; without fear if there seems no answering voice; nor troubled and uneasy if the hour of prayer seems long. But all is calm and still as the peace and presence of God breaks through the turmoil of the day. In silence he touches the hem of the garment of the living God.[3]

Silence can mean that the mind and body are reuniting themselves in therapeutic blends of wind, sand and stars.

There can also be something gracious about silence when it means the reluctance to condemn, as in the case of the woman at the well, or the home-returning son.

The other silences—what shall we call them?
The painful ones—
The ugly ones—
The empty ones—
Muteness in the presence of some life-damaging remark.

We don't need a catch-all label. It's enough that silence can be made of lead as well as of gold.

George Bernard Shaw called silence the most perfect expression of scorn.

As every family knows, if at breakfast father is unusually quiet, his silence does not mean that there is nothing wrong. Actually it may signify quite the opposite: father has something on his mind.

If you've ever had the "silent treatment," you know someone was trying to tell you something—that they resented you or that you had hurt them and they wanted you to hurt in the same way they did.

I've heard more than one marriage partner say: "If I try to talk, it always winds up in some nasty argument, so I just keep quiet. I don't say *anything*." What *that* means is: "I've found my own weapon—one with spikes in it—and I've decided to use it." Or, "This is a rotten technique I'm using to make my point, but I am justified in using it. I really am!" "If you knew my wife . . . ," or, "If you knew my husband . . ."

There's the earth-death silence of Rachel Carson's *Silent Spring*—losses that cannot be recovered.

And the silence with which death floods our worlds.

The night before a funeral service for a young mother, I went with the father and his three young children to the chapel where friends were coming to express their concern. Standing beside the casket with the family before anyone else arrived, I picked up one of the youngsters—a four-year-old blond—so she might see her mother lying there "asleep."

The little girl was aware, though, that this was strangely different. As I held her, she turned toward me and asked: "Can Mommy wiggle?"

Or we sense, in the silences of God, not his companionship, but a slowness to come to our aid. God's silence can hurt and burn—even make us angry at him. Can we feel better and function better if we say that?

In several of the Psalms voices importune: "God, say something to us! Show us you care! Speak!"

But all the sound that comes is the sound of sea water hitting the shoreline, or the wind bending a desert flower toward the ground.

Perhaps the most unwelcome silences are the ones that represent failure to speak when some wrong is in the process of being done. Someone we know is being maligned, and it's in our power to straighten out the record. But we don't.

Robert Louis Stevenson said, "The cruelest lies are often told in silence."

We have an obligation to lift up our voices in protest in the face even of minor wrongs. It's easy to cop out, to tell ourselves: "My job is to be a good citizen, to do what is right with my own life, and keep my nose out of other people's business." But can we be sure that's not evasion?

Someone who cares when *someone else's* rights are endangered, or when *someone else* is suffering from some condition that is subject to correction, is the mature person. To become involved in the security and the happiness of someone who owes us nothing, to spend something of ourselves for him—if nothing more than our inconvenience—to speak out on his behalf or risk our own disconnection by supporting him in his situation—that is what it means to be ethically grown up.

Churches which have shown the most growth in recent

years are those which seem to be narrow in outlook —exclusivistic, unwilling to become engaged in the human struggle at all. One way to get on the ecclesiastical success bandwagon seems to be to have little to say about hunger and schools, sexual confusion, economic justice, war or peace. Be against sin, and for the Bible, and the saints will come striding in. That kind of silence many of us still reject. We seek to be God's *inclusive* fellowship, not his *exclusive* one. We will not accept a Christianity that is maintained inside such a pietistic corral. The heart of the gospel is still not "save your soul" but "love your neighbor." We are of one loaf, and Christ belongs in our political debate as well as in our liturgy.

A student, just back from a big-on-showmanship evangelistic conference, had this to say:

> Jesus is the Word of God made flesh, sent to dwell among us; not some supernatural figure far removed from our earthly plight as human beings. The belief was often expressed at our conference that if only men could forget their worldly woes—like pollution and poverty, racism and war—and turn their eyes heavenward to Jesus, then all would be well; these grievous problems would resolve themselves. A strange attitude, I think, for those who claim to follow one who said he could be found, and served, among the "least of these, your brothers," among the poor and polluted, the victims of racism, war, injustice. Christian faith offers resources for dealing with social problems, not for escaping them.[4]

There's also the silence of those who take life, and use its gifts, but have nothing to say to the Giver in the way of grateful response.

I'm sure there are times when we wonder what the good

of worship is. We sing. So what? Say prayers. So what? Preach, listen to sermons. But who remembers them? Who cares, and so what?

There's an answer to this So What. It is that we will not accept the generosity of God and have nothing at all to say back to the One who gives us our life. Worship is at least some kind of awkward thank you, and that is better than silence.

In the Palm Sunday scenario, the Pharisees tell Jesus he ought to quiet the crowds, not let them make such a public fuss over his entry into Jerusalem. He replies: "If my disciples keep silent, the very rocks in the road will cry out."

In the heart of Appalachia there's a quaint little town called Pikeville, Kentucky. One of its best known hotels is the Hatcher. On its lobby walls are painted bits of mountain graffiti, thousands of proverbs, and notes of its historical happenings. One day there I read on the wall this statement: "Silence is the only substitute for brains."

Silence is the white space in the advertising of life. It's the force that gives indirect meaning to everyday's foaming waterfall of words.

To people who are compulsive "doers," silence is the summons to pull back from the temptation to assume absolute management of the world.

To the young, silence is a handle on the door of self-discovery.

To middle-agers, it's an antidote to hurry.

And to others full of years, it is a large cheerful room in which one never tires of wandering about, both in recall and in expectation.

There's a Lord of silence, too, who helps us keep our balance between the complementary worlds of adoration and action. Silence is but one more style of Yes. It can bless and steady us along our way with no more fanfare than that which accompanies a leaf turning colors, an uninhabited creek, an ant walking, children sleeping, time passing, a soft rainfall, or the first star coming out.

7. A full house is hard to beat

If you believe in Jesus, honk,
If you believe in love, do a handstand.
If you'd like to live forever, tell God.
If you want to be rich, wake up.
If you see ugliness, plant a seed.
If you see hunger, break your bread in two.
If you hate war, unclench your fist.
If you are afraid, look up; Sing!
If you are puzzled, welcome to the human race.
If you are searching for peace, stop.

James W. Angell

Almost everyone seems to be familiar with Southern California's star attraction Disneyland. Hollywood has long been known as Tinseltown, but Disneyland is regularly visited by presidents and kings. And now Florida has Disney World.

What everybody may not know is that the Disneyland of 1974 is different from the Disneyland of ten years ago. One development which has made it new and different is the adding of a Haunted House. My eleven-year-old Mary Scott and I visited it recently, touring the creaking, spooky old mansion in a two-seated car which moved from room to room on small guide rails. The scariest part came near the end of the ride when, as the car passed by a wall of mirrors, we noticed in looking at our reflection that there were *three* rather than two of us. The third passenger was a ghost!

Not all empty houses are haunted, but most haunted houses are empty. At least they are empty of people and the happy noises of families—chattering, eating, or practicing music lessons.

Jesus once told a story about a man who drove an evil spirit out of his life only to see the spirit return, bringing seven evil cousins with him.

We don't think of evil today in the same way our spiritual forefathers did, generations ago. But our experience *with* evil, plus a strangely reemergent Satanism, is fully enough to convince us that the subject matter of the Empty House parable is more than an obsolete fairy tale.

Hate is an evil spirit.

So is greed.

Feelings and attitudes which tear us down, pull us apart, are part of evil's destructive program.

The good spirits—of truth, love, beauty, and peace—are what hold us together. They are what give our lives unity and wholeness.

In everyone's life is "a place" where the war between goodness and evil goes on. In order to discuss this internal competition, we have sometimes spoken of evil as "the devil." This assumes evil is a part of our nature to be reckoned with. By speaking about a devil—giving this malevolent power on influence a mental form, even though imaginary—we have been able to focus on one of the oddest features of the universe: that man's biggest problem is himself. And Satanism as a form of reaction to earlier shallow optimisms, has lately made quite an impressive comeback.

Is the devil our latest hula hoop? Or is there in this discussion something that honestly challenges the modern mind? Is the devil more than some slang we use to blow off steam ("What in the devil do you think you are doing?")? Or do we have an adversary we'd better take seriously? Does the devil belong to the medieval world of superstition and witchcraft? Or is there something involved here that helps to explain a struggle which includes each one of us in its cast of characters—the struggle between hate and love, and violence and peace, death and life?

The world, and the history that goes on in the world, is not, according to the Christian Scriptures, simply a noisy street brawl without meaning, purpose, or goal. It is a world of critical choices—an unfinished world, a restless world, troubled by its vision of what it knows it ought to be, but can't achieve.

In the Old Testament the devil is pictured as a member of a celestial council who has God's permission to put man to the test. In the New Testament, Jesus, before undertaking his ministry, struggles with the devil in the desert. There the devil seems to be the Voice of Temptation and the provoker of a tough moral decision.

The virtue of Mr. Devil is that he helps make real to us the fact of choice. We cannot, without sacrifice, choose God and Love. And in a world and age wherein it is often intimated that all things are relative and that it doesn't make any really final difference what we do with our lives, or about them, this may be an important thing to say and believe.

What can we tell our children about evil? What can we tell ourselves?

We could begin here: Some would say evil is imaginary, and if people do wrong—if they kill or defame other human beings—it is because they are ignorant and "don't know any better." Or they haven't received a fair shake out of life; they

59

have lacked enough to eat, or to wear, or education, so they were deprived of a fair chance by a heartless, uncaring system. If everyone could be guaranteed a good chance at life, if everyone had a sound education and was clear about the difference between right and wrong, *that* would solve the problem.

Such an assumption, though, has a hard time proving itself to be true. Brilliant people still do "bad" things. Having ten-thousand-dollar cars to drive, ten-dollar steaks to eat, and ten million in the bank doesn't keep people from all kinds of errors. People still sin against the truth and goodness at the same time they know God wants something else from them. We still murder. We still hate, we still lie. And we still sell ours souls for plastic prizes.

We begin to ask why and to wonder if the devil isn't real after all. Not real like the Redwood forests or Tokyo, Japan. Not like our neighbor across the street, but as real as love, as real as anger, courage, or the sun. Perhaps if we have talked at times about the devil as if "he" were a visible fact or some enemy abroad in life, it is so that we might have a way to come to grips with a side of ourselves which everyone as he matures finds out he must wrestle against.

In the vacant house story we see a man who was successful in ridding himself of a bad influence in his life. We aren't told more than that, only that an evil spirit troubled him, and that he gained a victory by driving it out.

But that's all. He fumigated his life but was left a barren building. Clean, polished, proper. And sterile.

Like someone who could say: I don't do anything that's wrong. I don't drink. I don't cheat in my marriage or in my business. I don't lie. I don't swear. I don't kill. See how pure my life is!

Jesus says such a man imagines he is secure because he isn't violating any of the commandments. But he is not safe at all. He is in danger. God isn't primarily concerned with the things we do not do. He is far more interested in our yeses than our nos.

Unoccupied houses invite trouble. And many families now, when leaving on vacation, use an automatic switch to turn their house lights on and off in order to discourage any would-be vandals or robbers.

George Buttrick, preacher-scholar and author of the Matthew commentary in *The Interpreter's Bible,* wrote concerning this parable:

> An empty house, however it may be decorated, is always desolate. There are ghostly shadows at the windows. The floors creak. Every footfall echoes ominously. In the hollow distance there is the slamming of a door. Moreover, an empty house never remains empty. Spiders spin their webs, vermin claim the forsaken rooms, rats run behind the wainscoting—so our house of life left empty invites undesirable tenants. [1]

Full houses, on the other hand, can have a remarkable winsomeness about them.

A teenage son who bought a motorcycle was reluctantly allowed by his parents to take his first vacation alone across the country from the East Coast to the West Coast. He mailed postcards along the way, and the parents looked anxiously each time the postman came. But eventually he was safely back home, and he reported that one incident from his trip stood out among all others.

As he was traveling in North Dakota one day, he said, storm clouds were ahead and black ones behind, and he knew he was in for a drenching. He noticed about half a mile off the road a farmhouse with a large porch and a barn, so he made his way there and knocked on the door. A man and his wife met him. He asked if he could stay in the barn, but they insisted he come into their home. They gave him dinner and let him sleep in the guest room. The next morning he had breakfast with eggs and bacon.

Then, went his report, "before each meal they read the Bible and they prayed—real prayers including me. On the wall in the dining room there was a little embroidered design in a frame that said 'Jesus Be Our Guest,' and that is the way they treated me. Dad, they taught me more about God than I ever had known before."

In Pacific Palisades, California, at the ocean's edge, it is common to see houses built on the top of high hills. It is marvelous to live in one of those view-houses and each night to watch the sun sizzle into the sea, spreading out behind it a glittering freeway of gold. But some of the families who live in those houses have had problems. Land has crumbled away from beneath the foundations and left the homes hanging perilously from hillsides, with the result that many of them have had to be abandoned, wall murals, electric dishwashers, and all.

In the final sentences of the Sermon on the Mount (Matt. 6), Jesus comments on two kinds of places men choose to build houses.

One is on rock. Because such a house has a strong base it can stand up against any sort of violence.

The other is on sand. Houses built here cannot hold up when the winds and the tides press in against them. They are torn from their places, wind and water bouncing them about till they look like little mounds of toothpicks.

People need rugged foundations too, such as being *honest* in our personal relationships. If we are that, we never have to wonder if some third rider from the past will suddenly appear in the seat beside us or if we told one person one thing, another person something else.

And we must have centers of authority. When God is part of our value structure, misfortune and troubles lose their power to ruin us. Though there is much we do not know about God and so little that we do, we can still risk everything on that little in the same way we can speak over a telephone without understanding mysteries of electrical energy or watch a television set, knowing almost nothing about radio waves.

And we need the knowledge of forgiveness—how to offer mercy, how to accept it.

Then come bricks of hope, the mortar of patience, the reinforcing rods of discipline and sacrifice, polished glasses of wonder.

I called on Atina Nielson the other day. She is rich in years and has often shared with me interesting episodes from out of her nearly full century of living. On this particular visit she went to a small chest and brought out a tiny porcelain pot, small enough to be held between the thumb and forefinger. What fascinated me most, though, about this trinket was an inscription on the bottom. It said it was the reproduction of a bronze pot which had been discovered buried in the ground in Aberdeen, Scotland, almost a hundred years ago. And the pot had contained 12,267 silver pennies!

Who had saved them, and why? What ever happened to them? My thoughts reached out octopus-like for answers into a past that is unwilling to tell.

12,267 silver pennies! A thrifty Scot, no doubt. But life has been made to use—to be spent, traded. That's the only way to insure the fullness of living. And to see that our lives are "haunted," not by emptiness, but by the hunger to make them matter.

8. Our desperate hours can be managed

*A Saint is someone who has achieved a remote
human possibility. It is impossible to say what
that possibility is. I think it has something to
do with the energy of love. Contact with this
energy results in the exercise of a kind of balance
in the chaos of existence. A saint does not dissolve
the chaos even for himself, for there is
something arrogant and warlike in the notion
of a man setting the universe in order. It is a kind
of balance that is his glory. He rides the
drifts like an escaped ski. His course is a caress
of the hill . . . something in him so loves the
world that he gives himself to the laws
of gravity and chance.*

Leonard Cohen

The body of one young soldier killed in the Asian War was
brought back and buried in a cemetery in Van Nuys, which
is part of our huge San Fernando Valley. The boy's father
was deeply grieved by the loss of his son. One day, in the
extremity of sorrow, he went to the cemetery. Standing beside his son's grave, he pulled a pistol out of his pocket and
killed himself. That did not happen in a movie. It happened
in life, in 1971.

The skyjacker of a Frontier airliner, Ricardo Chavez
Ortez, made the price of surrender a chance to speak on the
radio for thirty minutes to ventilate the frustrations under
which he and his family were living. Without wanting to

confer approval on what he had done to dramatize his end-of-the-rope feeling, Chicanos nevertheless assembled, marched, and lobbied for clemency "because," they said, "we know how he felt; we feel and share most of the things he talked about, too."

What these two incidents have in common is desperation. Life at the breaking point. Human beings standing in the vortex of crisis.

What can we do about life's desperate hours? How can we help others, whom we care about, who find themselves in the midst of such awful emergencies?

"Thy arrows have sunk into me, and thy hand has come down on me" (Ps. 38:2).

"I am utterly spent and crushed . . . my heart throbs, my strength fails me; and the light of my eyes—it also has gone from me" (Ps. 38:8a, 10).

Concerning such exigencies Lofton Hudson says:

> Crises are times that try men's souls. They hit like a hurricane, or creep up and grab one's leg like an alligator, or pierce from within like a leg cramp or a charleyhorse, or dawn on a person like the sudden realization to a hunter that he is lost, one hour before dark.[1]

The crisis event may be a "Dear John" letter, a policeman at the door, a midnight conversation with one of our own children. Or, for millions of people in the world, it may be, what is there to eat? It may be some moment of unbearable guilt and shame, the tremor that shakes a family when there is the loss of a job, the wait for the doctor to come down from surgery to tell us how things are. Or maybe we just feel desperate about life generally, and aren't sure why. Its locus can be a college dorm, a family bedroom, a city street; or outer space, or maybe the White House.

Crisis is part of living, and faith needs to be storm-proof.
A friend in middle life, who had never had a great crisis,
but who had helped others through theirs, said:

> I have never been really hit hard by anything in life. I
> have had good health, never lost by death anyone very
> close to me. In fact, I have never been tremendously
> disappointed in a particular person. Maybe I expected
> the worst. But if a blow ever lands right in the solar
> plexus, I hope that, by the help of my friends and my
> faith, I will be able to stand up and take it.[2]

A daughter in her teens said, "Daddy, I don't think there
is anything that could happen to me in life that God and I
could not handle together. I believe that, whatever comes,
I could find a way to accept it and cope with it that would
be a reasonable and successful approach."

A crisis is not a signal to stop in our tracks altogether, but
it has been suggested that a good idea when all hell seems
to be breaking loose is to Stop, Look, and Listen.

What "stop" needs to stand for is rather that steadiness
of spirit referred to in Psalm 46:

> The nations rage, the kingdoms totter;
> Come and see, the desolations of earth.
> But God is still the refuge of men
> He makes wars to cease, he breaks the bow, he
> shatters the spear, he burns the chariots with fire.
>
> Be still, and know that I am God!

This is no sit-on-our-hands stopping of the kind that comes
when cynicism threatens to overpower us and persuade us
that life is no good, and that people are no good, that God
is no good. It is not the stopping of helplessness, but a

stopping that tells us we are not alone, the remembrance that in our desperation, God always stands near to uphold and to lead.

A crisis doesn't mean do nothing. It means that it's time to pause, time to seek those half-hidden resources for reaction which are part of our life in Christ.

Then look. Look for alternatives. Look for openings in the clouds. Look for Easter possibilities.

Faith is openness to God in the midst of each situation.

When we ponder what we are going to do, we are faced with questions like: What will people think? What am I able to stand? Will I die? Whose fault is this? Can I still go on after the storm is over? How do I attack this problem? Who can help me? If a person cannot find answers to *some* of these questions, he will be completely snowed.

A crisis doesn't end until we make a decision, take one of several possible roads, or until the event itself changes as a result of other circumstances.

The unwillingness to act, to do, to step forward and face the situation can immobilize us. If, at a railroad crossing, we were to sit there for hours looking and listening and never to get around to negotiating the intersection, the stop-look-listen warning would have backfired. That is not what it's meant to do.

We may be reluctant to elect between alternatives because we think we *might* choose wrong. To such fear our higher selfhood says: "That's right, you may *be* wrong. You may choose the wrong path. But that's okay. Don't be afraid to change your mind if that's what happens. You don't have to play God by pretending that you are always right."

Once a decision is made, crisis begins to dissolve. When we pass the point where events control us we can begin to manage the situation. We may not be on top of it. We may not be able to make things come out the way we would like them to come out, but something great will have happened. We will have proved something fundamental to ourselves. We are no longer afraid. We have an answer to the old riddle "Do you have a problem, or does the problem have you?"

And listen! Most of us flunk listening. Many of the songs written in this generation—"The Sounds of Silence," for instance—have told us how important it is for us to listen for what is going on in the lives of people around us, especially at the wordless levels of the heart where most of love's lasting transactions occur.

Listening is also one of the responsibilities of government. Government can't solve everybody's problems. The President of the United States has made an important point by saying that "throwing money at problems" doesn't solve them. But government must always attempt to understand and to feel.

In my counseling ministry, after I have talked with a person about a problem, he or she will frequently look at me and say, "I didn't expect you to give me an answer; it helps, though, to know that someone cares." That, for the moment, is enough.

Life isn't necessarily fair. It doesn't have to be, to be filled with glimmerings of the beautiful and the worthy. What matters more than anything else is the human spirit and its determination to "hang in there" regardless of circumstance.

A little less than a hundred years ago, Mark Twain, in a cynical mood, wrote a story called "The Great Catastrophe." Before he finished the story he worked all the characters into such a predicament that no matter what they did they'd end up losing. Then he closed the story by saying, "I have these people in such a fix that I can't get them out. Anyone who thinks he can is welcome to try."

That's the way things stood two thousand years ago.
Then He came, as Boris Pasternak put it,

> into Rome's tasteless heap of gold and marble . . . , light
> and clothed in an aura, emphatically human, deliberately
> provincial, Galilean, and at that moment gods and na-
> tions ceased to be and man came into being—man the
> carpenter, man the plowman, man the shepherd with his
> flock of sheep at sunset, man who does not sound in the
> least proud, man thankfully celebrated in all the cradle
> songs of mothers and in the picture galleries of world
> over.

Man came.

And God. God *in* man, so that man could discover the light
within himself and his lips could form the syllable Yes.

9. Transcendence is a kiss on the nose

You came so briefly
Went so quickly
We hardly knew
Whether we had seen you or
Not.

Still, you left us a name
A song of hope
A city to seek
And the memory
Of a
Star.

James W. Angell

cA young woman who committed suicide left this note: "I am twenty-one. I have seen everything worth seeing. I know everything worth knowing. I don't like life—it's cheap, dirty, disappointing. I've had all I want."

This is how to die hurting. It is to have missed the Yes dimension of life.

The Christian faith tells us there is more to living than meets the eye. That there's more to man than we can compress within the covers of a book on anatomy. And more to God than religion.

To the question "Is this *all* there is?" the Gospel answers: "No; there is more."

There are those who look upon this "more" discussion as

a way to anesthetize ourselves against the pain of truth. Faith, though, insists there *is* something—even though it says that it sees as "in a mirror."

During World War II, I rode a destroyer on antisubmarine patrol duty in the North Atlantic. Late one afternoon, excitement developed among the crew when the radio room shared a top-secret communication it had received. Within hours, it said, the *Queen Mary* would cross our path seven miles distant. On board, bound for Casablanca to confer with Winston Churchill and Joseph Stalin, would be President Roosevelt and his advisors.

At three the next morning we lined the rails with binoculars and long glasses. The moon was yellow as buttermilk. We waited, watched. Finally, the tip of a funnel ruptured the horizon. Then the full, toy-like, graceful silhouette, driving at flank speed on a southeasterly course. In less than ten minutes she was gone. Ours was only a glimpse, but enough to know the radiogram had been true. We had been involved in history.

Jesus moved briefly across the landscape, too, leaving behind the intimations of an eternal Order.

As children of Science, we are both impressed by and unsatisfied by our inventions. We are hungry for glimpses of something greater. Our age wants transcendence redefined.

Transcendence is life-enthrallment.

Wonder.

Hope's heart-beating!

A kiss on the nose, remembered forever.

Kennedy-style vision.

Bread.

The sea, the exhilaration of speed, the irrepressible energy of truth.

The cold majesty of a February snow.

Power that spins eight planets forward, one in reverse.

The sound of a mandolin at eleven o'clock at night.

Transcendence is the justice-yearning in man, forcing revolution; the forgiveness quality in God.

In the classical theological squabble of transcendence versus immanence, the question was whether God, in his creative role, stood apart from man and earth, or whether he was mainly knowable *in* Creation. One side said if God *made* the world, he couldn't be coextensive with it. The other side said the only god it could find was God revealed in the beauty of stars, the mystery of love, the sovereignty of conscience.

Belief in a God of magic and myth whose presence had to be evoked from outside led to the tendency to locate the divine points and mark them out as shrines and cults. The "transcendence" of God for many of us, though, has another meaning. It warns us against both word and wooden idols which tend to divert our attention from the need to be open to a Presence.

We seem more comfortable these days speaking about Jesus as the "Man for Others," whose "divinity" is not expressed as the One who enters from without, but whose love surpasses all other love so radically he becomes the *fullness* of God among us—fullness rather than differentness.

As astrology sweeps the sky today looking for signs of Yes, more and more people of no religion turn to horoscopes for guidance. Only 450 of the 1700 newspapers in America do not carry a daily article on astrology to meet public demands. Jean Dixon and Edgar Cayce are better known than Coretta King or John Gardner.

By contrast, the Church proclaims a message that God's Yes has already arrived.

To be strong within is to reach the conclusion that life's quality is more important than its quantity.

To be strong is to know that suffering can be purifying, and that life is often found by throwing it away.

To be strong is to know we're going to die, and that all people die. To be strong is to know we need other people's help, and that help is here.

Resurrection is a matter of glimpses, unpredictable breakthroughs of awareness. Of hours and days of unawareness and blindness, life-as-usual, so-what-else-is-new? Then, suddenly life is pierced by moments of surprise. The clouds part, and the subterranean meanings of our existence are revealed like fragments of diamond rock.

Peter Berger says such moments contain "signals of transcendence." They give us glints and gleamings of Another Realm.

The farther we proceed with social revolution, with our attempts to make the earth heavenlike, the surer we become that our faith in some realm of More Beyond has to be more than wish projection. The idea of heaven is rather the timeless concern which outranks even the vision of a smog-free planet, a guaranteed annual income, or a cure for cancer.

God is greater than our minds.

He will not adjust to our categories and definitions.

He will not confine himself to our system.

Yet, our hearts cry out to know. Our brains strain to believe.

The God who is a benevolent Giant somewhere out in space, or beyond space, doesn't satisfy our ground-floor hunger.

Neither does the idea that God is another name for Kindness or Freedom.

And faith remains a matter of sights half-seen—comets that race brilliantly across the sky, then are gone.

If this secret were not a secret, the thrill of living and striving would be lost. Perhaps it is part of the remarkable love of God that he makes himself difficult to find, that he gives us gauzy glimpses rather than daylight certainties.

Transcendence is a kiss on the nose

In Chaim Potok's *The Chosen* an old man is talking about his death to his son, Reuven. He says:

"I learned a long time ago, Reuven, a span of life is nothing. But the man who lives that span, *he* is something. He can fill that tiny span with meaning so its quality is immeasurable though its quantity may be insignificant. Do you understand what I am saying? A man must fill his life with meaning; meaning is not automatically given to life. It is hard work to fill one's life with meaning. That I do not think you understand yet, Reuven. A life filled with meaning is worthy of rest. I want to be worthy of rest when I am no longer here. You do understand what I am saying?" [1]

Is this all there is?
No.
Is there more?
Yes.

10. All you need to add is love

Each film, you see, has its moment of contact, of human communication: the line "Father spoke to me," at the end of Through a Glass Darkly; *the pastor conducting the service in the empty church for Marta at the end of* Winter Light; *the little boy reading Ester's letter on the train at the end of* Silence. *A tiny moment in each film—but the crucial one. What matters most of all in life is being able to make that contact with another human. Otherwise you are dead, like so many people today are dead. But if you can take that first step toward communication, toward understanding, toward love, then no matter how difficult the future may be— and have no illusions, even with all the love in the world, living can be hellishly difficult— then you are saved. This is all that really matters, isn't it?*

Ingmar Bergman
in a *Playboy* interview

William Yeats, referring to the first overwhelming but lost love of his life, wrote: "Everything I remember about her goes through me like a spear."

Like God, Love is an inexhaustible idea. We can talk and write about it forever, and it still winds up greater than any of our words or knowledge. It is the test of everything: of morality, of truth, of religion. It is part of our human experience which convinces us, more than anything else that happens to us, that there is a holy dimension to our living.

76

All you need to add is love

The demand to be loved is unrelenting. When that need is frustrated we will use every device we know to gain it, or we pay for the lack of it in fear, depression, or rage. In Western culture a person and his performance tend to merge. We are supposed to deserve love, or qualify for it by correct behavior; when that doesn't happen and we go unloved, we make these psychological retaliations.

"Agape" love—the unselfish love of one person for another —knows how to love even when performance is bad. It can still love and affirm the person, the fragile and precious self. This, and the fact that it also mirrors the quality of relationship we have with God, we have learned from Jesus.

The well-known writer Pearl Buck, who died in 1972, says of love: "It can't be forced; can't be coaxed or teased. It comes out of Heaven, unmasked and unsought."

Unless we can believe love is a miracle and not a pink candle on a sex cake, the universe turns out to be mostly a machine, and God a stale sentence in a stale book.

In her autobiography, *The Story of My Life*, Helen Keller tells how as a deaf and blind child she learned from Anne Sullivan the meaning of love.

> I remember the morning that I first asked the meaning of the word, 'love.' This was before I knew many words. I had found a few early violets in the garden and brought them to my teacher. She tried to kiss me; but at that time I did not like to have anyone kiss me except my mother. Miss Sullivan put her arm gently around me and spelled into my hand, 'I love Helen.'
> "What is love?" I asked.
> She drew me closer to her and said, "It is here," pointing to my heart, whose beats I was conscious of for the first time. Her words puzzled me very much because I did not then understand anything unless I touched it.

77

I smelt the violets in her hand and asked, half in words, half in signs, a question which meant, "Is love the sweetness of flowers?"

"No," said my teacher.

Again I thought. The warm sun was shining on us.

"Is this not love?" I asked, pointing in the direction from which the heat came, "Is this not love?"

A day or two afterward . . . the sun had been under a cloud all day, and there had been brief showers, but suddenly the sun broke forth in all its southern splendor.

Again I asked my teacher, "Is this not love?"

"Love is something like the clouds that were in the sky before the sun came out," she replied. Then in simpler words than these, which at that time I could not have understood, she explained: "You cannot touch the clouds, you know, but you feel the rain and know how glad the flowers and the thirsty earth are to have it after a hot day. You cannot touch love either; but you feel the sweetness that it pours into everything. Without love you would not be happy or want to play."

The beautiful truth burst upon my mind. I felt that there were invisible lines stretched between my spirit and the spirits of others.[1]

There are all kinds of meta-messages of love as people suffer, strive, and share life together, the bad and the good.

The Christmas story, says Helmut Thielicke, needs to be read on two levels simultaneously. The lower level—the bass clef—is the human side of things. There's an overpacked town to which people stream for the taking of a census, a shortage of accommodations with all its miserable side effects and gouging of citizenry. There's an expectant mother and a worried father, concerned for food, warmth, and safety. There are shepherds, some men from a passing caravan; national politics and a cold Judean wind. There is the mystery

78

of human life and suffering. Simple people and simple joy. Crowds and customers. Noise. The clop of camel feet, the sound of cattle switching their tails. Straw. Adults arguing. Children dreaming. The world turning. Night and day. Time and the river.

That, says Dr. Thielicke, is the bass clef. The lower line. The earthly dimension.

Above, in the upper register, angels are singing. In the treble clef God is active, his purpose working. Here tenor and soprano voices tell us something else is happening in history. A glistening, first-magnitude star is more than a star. It's a sign! And those men of the caravan with gifts for the baby—they are more than simply itinerant strangers: they are worshipers of a King. And Mary and Joseph are not just a peasant couple to be pitied because they are without a place to sleep. They are instruments of God's most daring intrusion into the most daring part of creation.

So we must talk, says Thielicke, when we tell the Christmas story, *both* about men and angels; earth below and heaven above; an event which is both part of time and which is greater than time. Only as both lines of the score are listened to together is there harmony, music almost too wonderful for hearing.

That's a pretty satisfactory way to describe what is going on in our own lives, all the time.

It's clear what happens when two people fall in love. There is the human dimension, the physical encounter, the planning for a life together, being together, touching. But if you're *really* in love, there's also an orchestra that's playing above your head, and you feel caught up in the grasp of one of the richest mysteries of being. And "the bread I ate with you was more than bread."

God even pops up in the middle of marriage. In Lois

Wyse's book *Love Poems for the Very Married* she has a verse called "Lines to an Unhandy Man":

> You never made
> A lamp base out of a Cracker Jack box,
> An extra room out of an unused closet,
> Or a garden out of a pile of clay
> All you ever made was
> A woman out of me.[2]

The world has a choice collection of four-letter words. In addition to those featured in the movies "for mature audiences only," there are words like care, kind, hope, and give. But the world's favorite four-letter word is love.

We are living in a time when we feel freer than most generations before us to acknowledge our love for each other, and that is a plus. In Victorian times love belonged strictly inside the relationship of family: husband for wife, wife for husband, parent for child. Outside, there was to be respect, honor, friendship, brotherhood. But love—that was a more guarded and restricted value.

Today's world is more open, more unstructured, at the same time more chaotic. But it is also probably more honest, and more full of promise in the long run.

And we must not give up on trying to build a society based on love as well as law.

Laws we must have. They are the bony skeleton of civilization. But we can have law books stacked as high as the Washington monument and still wind up a morbid and failed people.

An inner-city pastor named John Fry clashed with Mayor Richard Daley in Chicago and wound up being questioned by the McClellan committee of the Senate because of his efforts to work with the switchblade-wielding, dope-trafficking youth underworld of South Chicago. He said to his Presbyterian congregation on the Sunday following his return from his Washington interrogation: "So grow up and find out what our Lord was talking about. The most dangerous thing you can do is love. The world isn't ready for it. Greed it can manage. Lust it can understand. Hate it thrives on. Meanness makes it go around. But the world is enraged by love. So grow up and watch out."

A rebirth of trust is our most obvious need. Law and order may be a barrier separating us from the jungle. But it cannot make us a great people or a good people.

Life in God is life between two poles. It is the inward and outward journey combined. It is life which prays, "Dear God, give me bread *enough for today*"—not the next six weeks. It is life which appreciates its own restlessness as a gift which knows God is truth and truth is God. It is life which wears out, then is renewed. Life that dies, then explodes in resurrection.

In the play *A Hundred Years Old* by the Brothers Alvarez Quintero, an old man on his hundredth birthday asks his great-great-grandson:

"Trino, have you ever been in love?"

"Hundreds of times, Grandfather," Trino replies.

"Then you have never been in love."

The largest love story is that God loves you and I love you.

In the midst of that love there stands a cross, but it prevails.

It wins.

It overcomes.

It conquers the universe.

Death is not the last word in Earth's vocabulary.

Love is that word.

Recalling the forbidden interfaith marriages of the Old

Testament times suggests another marriage that was resisted by an obstinate father—that of Elizabeth Barrett in foggy, chilly London. But Robert Browning married her against her father's wishes and took his semi-invalid bride to sunny Italy to live. It was there, on an autumn afternoon, that Elizabeth Barrett showed her husband some sonnets she had written during the family-troubled courtship but never told him about. He thought they were beautiful, and he wanted the world to see them, but she thought they were too private. His nickname for her, because of her dark brunette hair, was "my little Portuguese." Eventually those poems were published as *Sonnets from the Portuguese.* The best known begins: "How do I love you—let me count the ways. . . ."

We can't all write verse for the world to remember us by, but we can all love. No one is denied that possibility. Nothing else matters very much.

"Yes is a world . . ." wrote e. e. cummings, remember? And

> love is a place
> & through this place of
> love move
> (with brightness of peace)
> all places [3]

11. What shall we do about the problems we can't do anything about?

Sometimes as parents or grandparents or ministers, when we feel that we have done all that we humanly can, and that we must take our hand off and back away, is there not one thing more we ought to do by word and attitude? Do we not have to make it clear that our love will not let go—that the door will always be open—and that the upstairs window will bear the "nose marks" of one who never gives up believing that some day a familiar figure will be seen trudging homeward?

Bill, a good friend

What shall we do about the problems we can't do anything about?

That may sound like a foolish statement: contradictory, ridiculous. Admitting this, though, doesn't remove from us the dilemma we frequently face of wanting to do something to change a situation, or of wanting to help another person to change his situation, yet knowing that it is probably something beyond our power.

Perhaps the happiness of one of our children is involved. He or she faces a major decision which he or she alone must make. Or some problem which will have an important effect upon the future. They are down on themselves, or in the midst of a divorce, or have dropped out of college, gotten deeply in debt, or have become destructively involved with drugs or alcohol.

We want to help; w᠌ try to help, but we know that there is a limit to our ability to resolve their problem. We cannot be happy for someone else, or believe in God for someone else, or make certain important decisions *for* someone else, without annihilating their freedom, their selfhood, their dignity. We are up against one of those problems it seems that we can't do anything about. Having done what we can, we reach a point where we can't do any more. We can only watch from the sidelines and pray.

I knew a young man who was continually being apprehended by the police for petty crimes. Each time he wound up in jail, his grandmother came to the rescue. She would put up the bail, pay the damages, or do something else to backstop her grandson's mistakes, so Robbie never wound up accepting responsibility for his own life. His grandmother meant well. She was a fine woman—a caring, compassionate person; but responsibility was a problem Robbie himself had to learn to face. He never did.

Or, we can turn the story around and paint a different picture. This time it's not a child, but a parent, at the center of concern, and the one who is doing the worrying is a devoted son or daughter. It could be an aged parent—immensely loved. But time has imposed its taxes, and the parent is experiencing failing health, or is lonely for a lost mate, or has reached the place where life seems empty and pointless, little more than a burden.

The adult son or daughter wants to help, to relieve the pain, to bring some of the life-quality he or she is experiencing into that life that has meant so much in the years that have gone by. But again, there are limits to what one can do. Then one must leave the matter with God.

What shall we do about the problems we can't do anything about?

Blowing this dilemma up to larger scale, we recognize that the world itself often seems to be put together unfairly. We see conditions we long to change. We yearn to see an end to mental illness, starvation, war, racism. (Fortunately there are still a few angry people who are willing to lay their lives on the altar of public contempt to produce change—at least a partial end to old wrongs which have tormented life through the ages.) But we still must make peace, somehow, with the world as it is, or we will burn ourselves out in despair and wind up changing nothing. The message of Christianity is that though we may not be able to do everything, we can do *something*—something that will make a difference, that will give our lives a few moments of radiant significance.

Yet another category of problems exists: the staggering enigma of our mentality—our inability to control those decisions on which the deepest joy of our lives depends. When we lose a loved one, we must accept that. We hunger for a miracle which could back up the clock and run that part of our lives through again—and make our lives come out with a different result. But it cannot be. We can have no inward rest at all—none—until we accept what has happened.

> You can't unring a bell,
> You can't unshine a star,
> You can't retrieve a word you've said—
> The things that are, just are.
>
> But you can accept the truth,
> You can breathe deep and free,
> You can, out of emptiness, create
> A fact, and a flame, called Me.

JAMES W. ANGELL

85

Not just death. The whole rushing river of time. The cross of Christ. The failures of yesterday.

"The moving finger writes, and having writ, moves on," and all our tears and all our wit, can't wash out half a line. . . .

The past we cannot change. Neither, though, are we helpless in the face of that truth, nor without hope.

"What shall we say to these things?" asked Paul, after he had documented the love of God and then tried to match *that* truth up with the brutalities and irrationalities that still make up much of the news in our daily newspaper.

Something we *can* do is to learn to accept our finiteness and our humanness. That's no small assignment, and it isn't an answer that won't come unglued, once we think we've got it put together. It will. But acceptance of the tentativeness and perishability of life is a grace that can be mastered gradually. No one can learn to play the piano in a week, and no one can find out what it means to be a Christian in a year. This is why God gave us the Church: so that we could have a place to grow and mature.

We must find a way to come to terms with the fact that we are not gods, but the children of God. Our knowledge is fractional, our victories conditional, and our happiness is, intentionally, I suspect, incomplete in this world and this life.

It's hard to admit that we cannot manage the world nor control all outcomes. It's difficult to "let go and let God," and it's difficult to set each other free—especially our children. But this we must do.

We are not invincible. We are men. We blunder, receive forgiveness, try again. And we will live in hell if we go through life making perfectionist demands of ourselves. We must accept life—its ambiguities along with its sublimities.

We must see its problems not just as inconvenient intrusions, but as occasions for living out who we think we are. When we are able to solve a problem, we feel good—useful. When we can't solve it, we reach out to each other for help and for comfort, and for reassurance that life isn't picking on us. Slowly our strength and courage and our interest in the future returns.

We will not get answers to all our perplexities but we will turn into men and women in whom God delights if we can allow life's weather to shape us into exhibits of the kind and the brave: trees, planted by the rivers of water, bringing forth the fruit of the Unafraid Life.

We can pray for our children, and love them, and listen to them at the same time that we free them so that they, too, can grow through an awareness of their own morality and dependency upon God and faith. If we have older parents we care about, and want to make life richer and easier for them, we must concede them also the right to be who they are. We must recognize that, while being young and vigorous is a wonderful thing, it is not the only thing that deserves to be called beautiful or right.

And when we come to the place where we must make our own rapprochement with death, we must make it as part of the larger truth we have been talking about, that life is more like a flower than a steel building; more like a kiss than a paid-up insurance policy.

Norman Vincent Peale tells a story about a young man who grew up in impoverished circumstances, at least as they would be defined today—but not poverty of spirit, only of material goods. His widowed mother operated a small general store in a remote neighborhood, and she scrimped and saved to give her son the best possible chance for a favorable life of his own. When he was ready to go to college, she

87

dug out from underneath her mattress a bunch of crumpled twenty-dollar bills she had been saving for that day. When that mother died, said Dr. Peale, the son found his sorrow more than he could handle.

He kept brooding over it. His mother had had so little, it seemed. She had sacrificed so much for him, and now she was gone. Then, says Dr. Peale, one winter's day, he went out to the cemetery, stood beside her grave, and said aloud: "Mother, I am going to let you go. You've earned peace, happiness, reunion with Dad. Mother, I am letting you go." And for the first time, the knot inside him seemed to dissolve.*

"Be patient toward all that is unsolved in your heart," wrote Rainer Maria Rilke, "and try to love the questions themselves."

We cannot allow the limitations of our humanness to crush the joy and the excitement out of us, for we are also called to Love and to the immediate! The part of the riddle of life which is within our reach is shot through with the divine already. Life is not a problem to be solved; it is a mystery to be lived.

The psychiatrist Viktor Frankl survived many harrowing experiences in Nazi prison camps, and it has been said about his writings that "they rest on experiences too deep for deception." He tells how in one of those first post-war years, after he had resumed his medical practice, a rabbi from an Eastern country came to him and told him of losing his first wife and their six children in the concentration camp at Auschwitz. It turned out that the rabbi's second wife could not have children, and he lamented that there would be no son of his own who could ever say Kaddish for him after his death. But Frankl decided that his anguish had deeper roots.

---

* From the book *A Guide to Confident Living* by Norman Vincent Peale. © 1948 by Prentice-Hall, Inc. Used by permission.

"I made a last attempt," he writes, "to help him by inquiring whether he did not hope to see his children again in Heaven. However, my question was followed by an outburst of tears, and now the true reason of his despair came to the fore: he explained that his children, since they died as innocent martyrs, were found worthy of the highest place in Heaven, but as for himself he could not expect, as an old and sinful man, to be assigned the same place. I did not give up, but retorted: 'Is it not conceivable, Rabbi, that precisely this was the meaning of your surviving your children: that you may *become* worthy of joining them in Heaven? Is it not written in the Psalms that God preserves all your tears? So perhaps none of your sufferings were in vain?'" [1]

Dr. Frankl says that, for the first time in many years, the man found relief.

It becomes easier to cope if we believe nothing in our experiences is wasted. It is not hardship but the feeling that nothing ultimately matters that crucifies us.

When at age twenty-one my own daughter Susan was killed in an automobile accident, I felt as if the cross of Jesus I had spoken about in pulpits for many years had suddenly become internalized. The cross was no longer something suspended in the chancel; now it was something within my heart.

"It is a tremendous moment" says George Romanes, "when first one is called upon to join the great army of those who suffer. That vast world of love and pain opens suddenly to admit us one by one within its fortress. . . . Since Christ, this world of pain is no accident untoward or sinister, but a lawful department of life, with experiences, interests, adventures, hopes, delights, secrets of its gates—things that we could never learn or know or see, so long as we were well." [2]

Jesus, in Gethsemane, was up against a situation he felt

helpless to change, so he prayed, "Nevertheless, *your* will be done." That prayer changed the world. A light came on and it continues to shine. Perhaps the real answer to the question we have raised in this chapter is that there is nothing, really, in life of which it must be said: "That's something we can't do anything about." It just seems that way.

12. Yes ma'am

*Father: So you lost the spelling contest.
Who beat you?*

Son: A girl named Margaret.

Father: A mere girl!

*Son: Maybe you don't know it, Dad, but
girls aren't so mere any more.*

ⒶAbigail Adams used to complain to John that he and his colleagues in the Continental Congress talked glibly enough of liberty but failed to extend its benefits to their own wives.

That charge has sprung to life again in this decade with new fervency, and anyone who knows anything about women knows important social changes are in the works.

The basic agenda is correct. Ethically right. Unstoppable. Consistent with a slowly evolving humanization of persons and relationships. And if "Women's Lib" has a radical van which, at times, seems kooky and irresponsible, that should not obscure the reality that a majority of the women, both of America and the wider world, have already begun to feel a

91

rustle in their souls and to share the vision of a truer future for themselves as human beings. These changes also involve, of course, the family, sexual mores, laws, education, the shape of governments.

Los Angeles has adopted a "unisex" policy for its police force, which means that no longer are there some jobs for men, and others for women, that there is but one set of jobs for whomever qualifies. Constitutions are being rewritten. The term "chairperson" (rather than "chairman") is even beginning to sound slightly natural.

Like it or not, Right-to-Life movement or not, abortion is earning respectability.

And what would our grandparents have thought of a conversation like this?:

Teacher: "I am planning to arrange for a conference with Billy's father."

School principal: "I don't believe that's Billy's father. I think it's a relationship, not a marriage."

Does this add up to moral breakdown, or the dawn of a healthier tomorrow?

While there are no simple answers, we're ready to cast a few votes.

The main thrust of the women's movement is Yes, because it says Yes to personal freedom and self-determination. Whatever enhances the fulfillment of persons is of God. It is possible to wipe out unfair discrimination *without* wiping out differences. And laws which free women to attain and compete on equal terms in the marketplace of life have Justice as their ally.

This is not to undervalue home and family and the splendid dependency of men and women symbolized in the story of Adam's rib—the father-mother-child triad which has formed the cornerstone of civilization as we have known it and made most of us what we are. Does Women's Lib add up to a rejection of the sanctity of life and love, shared bodies, shared sufferings, shared dreams?

The answer is not yet reportable. But many believe it is possible to say Yes to the new image of Woman in our time and simultaneously to say Yes to the precious things we continue to identify with home and spiritual marriage.

Good homes are not always the result of a woman who is committed to staying there and dusting furniture, cleaning the bathroom, entertaining at bridge, and having hot meals ready when other members of the family come charging in from school or office. An engaging portrait, perhaps, but it does not assure the presence of happy, unfrustrated, loving, trusting individuals. And though such a pattern of living may have been ideal in 1920, the change which has permeated every inch of life since then—bringing trauma and revolution to communications, transportation, medicine, education, politics, and religion—has forced us to rethink what it will mean to be a family in the early twenty-first century, or a whole person within a family.

But home is an attitude, more than a life-style or a mortgaged Cape Cod. What is somewhat new in our day is the discarding of the notion that the woman member of the family is the manager and main attitude-center of the home, that *she* runs it and sustains it for the benefit of all the family members.

There are two reasons for the change. One is technology, for homes today are managed by dollars rather than by "homemakers." Oh, things still get dirty and there's the laundry, marketing, chauffeuring and all that. There's do-it-yourself fixing and the lawn. But money and machinery have worked important changes in what a home-centered woman is expected to do, or even *can* do, to make her hours matter.

The second is the acceptance by most men, under the new order, of coequal responsibility to guide and guard children and to help the home function as a place and process for the creative, happy encounter of persons, all of whom have gifts and all of whom have needs.

It is possible to say Yes to women as liberated persons and also to say Yes to the home, if we concede that home-*making* is not the responsibility of one member of the family but conjointly of all.

In the 1940s, when because of World War II hundreds of thousands of women went to work, there was clearly a flight from the home. A national emergency justified it, and electric dishwashers and TV baby-sitters made it possible. There followed an accelerating economy. Two-, then three-car mobility. Easier divorces. And automated manufacturing, meaning jobs requiring more brain than brawn (thus more opportunities for females). Families tended to become unglued and the home to lose its significance and moorings.

That stage of temporary abandonment is ending, and the home is being rediscovered as the locus of much of life's richest pleasure and meaning.

Formerly, where one worked was where the action was. Home was where we went to rest up so we could return to the battle sixteen hours later. But with work becoming increasingly a matter of circuitry and paper-shuffling in some distant metropolitan antiseptic-atmosphered high-rise, office romances which usually had dismal outcomes and the five o'clock drink becoming increasingly boring also, home has tended to re-emerge as the new center where the most excitement happens.

Page Smith of the University of California at Santa Cruz wrote the following in the *San Francisco Chronicle:*

Yes ma'am

[Home] is the one place where we can enact the drama of our own reality, where we are ourselves, free of those debilitating distortions of reality that most of us experience as our "work."

The flight from home is thus a flight from ourselves —from our own barrenness, inattention, unimaginativeness, unlovingness—to the spiritually numbing distractions of most jobs and careers, to a world of ceaseless motion, restlessness, misplaced ardor, false hopes, all the illusions of power and success of which our culture is so prolific.

Today, nevertheless, the home—which should be a center of peace and joy, of the classic domestic delights that have sustained life for centuries—is depicted as a prison cell, the abode of a boredom only slightly relieved by the pale blue flicker of television; or, more commonly perhaps, by a bedlam of squabbling children, unmade beds and unwashed dishes, presided over by a mad housewife, tranquilized twice daily, tending to dipsomania.

I don't want to "condemn" anyone to the home, man or woman. But I have a settled conviction that a man's and a woman's place is in the home.[1]

Children, too, are the richer for having as mothers women who, while they have substituted skiing for scrubbing, find there are new things they can now give their sons and daughters because of the new feelings they have about themselves.

The Church can and must say Yes to the New Woman and to the Home (not as woman's domain but as a movable Feast wherein all give, all receive); Yes to the divinely intriguing difference between being a man or a woman. Yes to laws which remove the temptation to exploit women through lower pay and which clear the way for women to move smoothly and productively into the economic and political spheres. Yes to enduring marriage, grounded in thought-out commitments and sustained by trust, growth, and mutual stimulation, not just by lawful sanction. Yes to mothers who tuck their children into bed with goodnight kisses and Yes to women who still believe that "wife" is a proud and a pleasant, not a peasant, word. Yes to the dignity and rightness of being single. Yes to women who champion the cause of *all* women, including large numbers who must work because others depend upon them, women who are widowed, who are black and experience double-struggle, and those who know the bitterness of poverty and poor health because they were part of an old order where their role as domestics and baby-havers were their chief reasons for being alive at all.

Organized Christianity deserves some of the credit for the changes which are taking place in our lifetimes, but also some of the blame for making them so late.

The long tale of a God who is male, a Redeemer who is male, teachings which say that the husband is the head of the wife and a male-dominated Church—what all of this reveals about God's intentions for the human family—is too complex to disentangle here. Let us settle for this: Jesus is our Liberator as well as our Lord. "There is no such thing as Jew and Greek, slave and free man, male and female; for you are all one person in Christ Jesus" (Gal. 3:28, NEB). Liberation is an open-ended process. It has led the People of God through innumerable changes. In our human understanding —of Christ, the Bible, sin, and the nature and destiny of man and woman. To attempt to make out our case for the old order, or the new, by proof-texting the Scriptures (choosing particular verses to support a predetermined conclusion) is silly and of no use to anyone who rejects that method for getting at the truth. What Jesus offers us—and has always offered us—is a Spirit, not a System. If we cling to that, the institutional Church will be part of the future's Yes where *both* men and women are concerned.

Where we shift from Yes to No is in the refusal to resolve these role adjustments in terms of conflict between the sexes: in terms of women's hatred for men or men's disdain for women. Men and women are persons *before* they are either men or women.

No, too, to those who would wipe out the ancient virtues of courtesy, gentleness, and simple kindness; man's instinct for protectiveness; woman's magnificent ability to be tender. No to that coarse view which makes intercourse only selfish gratification and not the mystical communication of self and love for another.

No to whatever downgrades the mystery and the glory of men and women being created by God to bless and complement each other.

A group of women were asked to answer the question: What do you immediately think of when you hear the term "women's liberation"? These are the responses which filled the blackboard:

> Gloria Steinem
> Women's movement
> militant
> irritation
> no bras
> youth
> freedom
> finally!
> challenge
> sisterhood
> new thinking

anti-motherhood
healing
equality
state of mind
misdirection
radical
intrinsic value

After a lifetime of casting about the depths of female psychology, Sigmund Freud made this entry in his diary: "What do women want; my God, what do they want?"

The answer, by now, is clear: They want to be free as men are free. They want to fulfill their potential and realize their own identities. They want political, economic, and social equality they believe is denied them by tradition and masculine coercion.

It took women fifty-two years of campaigning to get the right to vote. Today, women want more than that. They want their humanity acknowledged.

Senator Sam J. Ervin, who chaired the Watergate investigations, and who is widely recognized as a civil libertarian, has been one of the chief congressional opponents of the Equal Rights Amendment ("Equality of rights under the law shall not be abridged by the United States or by any state on account of sex") because he said such a change would "repeal the handiwork of God."

Those, though, who hope to harvest the best of the present intersexual ferment see that kind of result as the opposite of their goal. There are, doubtless, those who have no interest in the religious implications of such reassessments—but see them only in hard political terms. For others, it is part of our total growing up into the full maturity of being. We are like operators of derricks, lifting huge granite blocks of history and tradition about and trying to set them in their right new locations without causing the Temple of Life to come crashing and smashing down.

For most of us the matter is more than simply academic. Our daughter Mary Scott will soon cross over from childhood into adolescence. I want for her the same benedictions of being which I found in my mother and enjoy in the woman to whom I am enthusiastically married. For Mary Scott I want no less, but possibly more—more of the new freedoms latent in the new Tomorrow.

When we are small, the ambiguities—and the contradictions—of the life process don't get to us. The world seems rather sensibly put together. There are seasons. The sun rises and sets on schedule. The larks sing. There is moonlight for making love, there are lakes for swimming, and there is food on our tables. But then we begin to get acquainted with the tough realities that start to burn away our optimisms like spreading acid. The scales start to tip in a down direction. We get introduced to human corruption and have to begin to take seriously tragedies that tour in out of nowhere, leaving our ships with big holes in their sides, sinking.

It takes Jesus of Nazareth to liberate us from the conclusion that life is cruel and without final meaning.

He also liberates us from resignation and helplessness. He shows us there is a better response we can make to life than complaining about its lack of justice. He calls us to original gallantries of our own. Because of him we are no longer locked inside closed systems of rules and customs. Instead we are changed into a people who sing about a love that will not let us go, that will not let us down, and that will not let us off.

And he introduces us to the life of grace.

In Los Angeles, near the Sheraton, there's a parking lot that advertises rates of so much per hour. If you leave your car there while you do errands and it takes that hour to get them done, but it turns out to be an hour and five minutes before he can get back to the lot, he still pays for only the single hour's parking. But an hour and seven minutes is a different matter. Then he must pay for the extra time. The first six minutes, though, are free.

Six minutes is also the amount of time allowed in operating rooms after a cessation of heart action, before brain damage and/or death occurs. If a patient's heart stops on the table, there are but six small precious minutes available to save life.

Grace is the life of Yes—and freedom. It is celebration rather than obligation. It has stopped trying to prove or pay its own way. It is too busy enjoying being alive.

If we can keep this in mind, the future can be embraced by persons, and by families, without anxiety or fear.

It seems certain to be filled with continuing experimentation: limited-term marriage, acceptance of the right of a woman to bear and raise a child without the necessity of marriage, single adult communities, "group" marriage—these and other variations on the theme that people need people.

Love, though, can be counted upon not to change much. And if we keep our eyes on that Star we're certain not to get lost.

13. Dancing on a battlefield

Dance, dance, wherever you may be
For I am the Lord of the Dance said He.

cA motel in the vicinity of Gettysburg, Pennsylvania, advertises: "Sleep on the Battlefield." That may be a rare experience of fantasy where the battlefield has fallen quiet, but battlefields where people presently live and die and hunt for human significance are anything but quiet.

Life is war, even if it did have its beginning in a garden of chirping birds.

It is great theater, a journey of wonder, a crucible.

Occasionally it is a pineapple sundae. Other times it is Gethsemane—sweating resistance against despair—where to have any chance at all we have to put on the "whole armor of God."

Life is filled with ecstasies—and morgues. It must be, if it includes flowering pear trees on a March morning, mass murder at My Lai, and leukemia in Louisville.

Battlefields are mostly for killing. But they could be used for dancing, for some choreographed word about man's stunning possibilities, for a ballet of belief.

Battlefields have had various names: poverty, heroin, unemployment, homosexuality, mental depression, and loneliness. Hill Number Six, Kent State, and Attica.

Life derives some of its shine from the fact that it takes so much guts to cope with it. William James wrote:

> Mere ideals are the cheapest things in life. The more a man has the more contemptible he is if there have been no scars incurred, no pains accepted in the effort to have them realized.[1]

Author Anne Douglas Sedgwick, writing from a hospital bed, as life drained from her body sometime around her fortieth year, spoke to her own heart in these words: "I am thankful I lie in the hands of God."

Loss of faith is Thermopylae, Waterloo, Appomattox, and Remagen Bridge rolled into one. But as long as what we are fighting for, or fighting against, has meaning, we can get the hell kicked out of us and still not lose that light in our eyes.

How, though, can we "keep on keeping on" or come up with those five extra minutes of faith when life behaves as irrationally as it often does? How can we navigate the hard agenda of Holy Week and come out on the Easter side?

One way is to practice living the grateful life—the life of unconditional thanksgiving.

Thankfulness is a habit. A life style. Life freshened by the lilt of personal gladness. It is an emotion which displaces other negative forms of feeling and thinking.

Have you stood beside a service-station pump watching your gasoline tank being filled? If so, you may remember seeing a tiny column of air rush out of one side of the tank opening as fuel flows in the other. There isn't room for both.

A Los Angeles area psychiatrist came up with a suggestion in case of an earthquake: become angry; lash out at the earth; demand that it stop shaking; stomp your feet if you're able to stand up. His theory: anger and fear cannot coexist. He contends that anger can and will replace fear and that we are better off mad than afraid.

Gratitude is the core of Christian worship, and regularly we come saying: "God, thank you. Thank you for life and breath and hope. Thank you for yourself. Thank you for myself. Thank you that there is something inside of me that wants to say thank you. Thank you that when my world of happiness seems to go up in flames, you stand beside me to assure me of your love and support."

Here's an exquisite letter a mother received from her college-age daughter:

Thank you for seashells and skirt hems, for answers and orange juice. Thank you for questions and fresh curtains and eternal understanding. Thank you for wonder. Thank you for climbing the stairs to my room. Thank you for candles, shining copper pans and the smell of pine boughs. Thank you for listening to "My Fair Lady" 5,000 times. Thank you for kitchen-table talks and cartoons on the bulletin board. Thank you for listening and trusting. Thank you for making a home alive with ideas and music and fresh flowers. Thank you for chocolate-chip cookies and getting angry. Thank you for reminding me to clean out the bathtub and for picking up my shoes. Thank you for growing up beside me and always ahead of me.

Thanksgiving is the minuet by which we declare ourselves in favor of life. It enables us to sing songs at midnight while in jail. To join a universe in motion. To become part of that motion, part of God.

Love and faith are not abstractions. They are leaping relationships, harmonies that flow. They cannot be squeezed inside a fist or studied under a microscope. They are imperishable, always perishing.

If it seems ridiculous to thank God when all the stars seem to have disappeared from our sky, this is a no harder-to-accept ethic than what we might expect from a king whose coronation occurs in the form of a murder at the city dump!

Dr. Harry Emerson Fosdick wrote:

> Our life itself is an enigma, and it takes an enigma to meet its need. What good would Christianity be to us today if it were centered and confined in the lovely stories of Bethlehem, with adoring wise men and shepherds and singing angels? This is no adequate representation of what life confronts us with. Life is a mysterious, baffling, often tragic enigma, and the cross, which is an enigma too, talks to our true estate—a huge historic tragedy that yet takes in you and me, a revelation of man at his worst that can happen that yet turns the best to the brave. . . .[2]

Halyburton, a Scottish saint, said: "I have found a law that always, even when at the lowest deeps, I can pull myself back into the sunshine through the duty of thankfulness."

That is one way to cope when life tastes, not like champagne, but vinegar.

In his *Feast of Fools*, Harvey Cox retraces the history of religious dance and sees its return to the worship setting as a plus, one of the weapons of joy we can and must use against the enemies of negation. "What eventually happens to the

Church or to liturgical dancing is not a matter of urgent concern in itself," he says. "What happens to our stifled, sensually numbed culture is important." [3]

A dance is unlike a painting in that, when it is over, it ceases to "be." Even with "instant replay," its magic isn't the same. Like moonbeams, it "can't be carried home in a jar."

Above our town are some majestic peaks which, through a half-dozen months of the year, are topped with snow. The highest and best known is Mt. Baldy. On a clear day this mountain is brilliantly visible from Los Angeles, forty miles away. During a brief part of the winter, at around five every afternoon, the sun hits the summits in such a way as to turn them pink. Not rose hued, but hot pink. The pink snows last less than five minutes. If one is busy inside over a stove, or driving south on the freeway, he is apt to miss them altogether. As easily do we miss the splendor of life as it dances by, a hand extended in our direction.

Over the last ten years or so, most of us, whether we've wanted to or not, have been keeping score on the number of McDonald's hamburgers that have been sold. If I'm up to date, the latest total is thirteen billion.

A billion is a lot.

A billion is so many your mind can hardly take it in.

The earth, for example, is only 4.6 billion years old.

I've also heard it put this way: if you opened a business with a billion the day Jesus was born and lost a thousand a day ever since, it would *still* be another eight hundred years before you were out of money.

The number of people in the world today is between two and a half and three billion and growing. In the United States we add, every thirty days, enough people to populate a new city the size of Omaha, Nebraska, or Richmond, Virginia. That's net growth.

Not all people are the same, and everybody in the world

doesn't want the same things out of life. Still, it is amazing how many different ways people can find to dance the dance of life, whether they live in Teheran or Tuscumbia. Working and dreaming. Suffering. And hoping. Loving and lying. They watch the weather, have their days of festival. They pray and play. They grieve and wonder.

The battlefields of the '70s still include troubled teenagers, the lonely aged, uprooted migrants, the hidden poor. And the hope of these years is a gospel that still calls upon each one of us to become an agent of reconciliation. It calls upon persons to dance upon the battlefield of the world because there was a Man who did that—who never minimized the pain and the problems of people or forgot about them, but who never forgot, either, that life is a fragile appointment with beauty, a magnificent chance, a blue and yellow kite supported by the sweet laughter of an April wind.

14. Alternative to buying a wig

A New Year's no good
By itself but
Any old day will do
If you ring in
The new me.

—David Redding

In Santa Barbara, I walked one night along the beach. There in that city of blue and creamy charm, in the midst of my walk, I stopped in front of a wig shop. Through the lighted front window, a sign caught my eye: "Buy yourself a wig—it's the quickest way to create a new 'you.'"

If a wig can help you feel new about yourself I'd say: go get one. A look at what the Church calls "new life" through faith may, however, furnish another interesting possibility.

Such new life does not provide insulation from the roughness of the world. But it believes God is there—always there—like sun behind fog, or twenty-four-hour stars that only stand revealed as night falls.

Often, new life emerges in the midst of conflict, not as a protection from it.

Sometimes people say: "I don't believe any more. Once I did, but I have lost faith."

I have heard that a thousand times, and not as idle chatter. When people say this, they mean every word of it. What is happening, though, is not that they have really lost everything. Rather, they are moving through the choppy waters of the necessary struggle that will carry them, in time, into new harbors both of wisdom and compassion.

The world can do many things to us. It can excite us, amaze us, challenge us. But it can also embitter us, deceive us; crush us by its unreasonable weight.

Wrote William Wordsworth:

> The world is too much with us; late and soon;
> Getting and spending, we lay waste our powers:
> Little we see in Nature that is ours;
> We have given our hearts away. . . . [1]

Vacations help correct that. A good night's sleep helps us correct it, faith helps us to correct it. Jesus often "went apart" to lonely places—often up into the hills. And we know prayer can help us to correct and contradict those May and June views of the world and life which come out tired and shopworn, pessimistic and negative.

Shall we state the human equation in terms of wind, sand, and stars or schoolbooks, price-freezes, and the laundry? Both describe part of life, something needful. We have needed both our Thoreaus and our Van Brauns. The most serious mistake we could make would be to say that life is one or the other. Life is the dynamic which emerges when two truths are crossbred or treated as two hemispheres of a single wholeness.

The renewing of our minds occurs in the process of moving back and forth between the worlds of hang-loose and hang-tight. All work and no play makes Jack a dull boy. All play and no work also makes Jack a vain, self-centered slob. If we make a mistake by never taking time away from the familiar, we make just as serious a mistake by not coming back to lives of duty and involvement, sharing in the tasks of repairing and renewing the humanity of all men.

There is a principle of alternation involved here—a principle which seems built into the fabric of almost everything. There are day and night. Joy and sorrow. Summer and winter. Youth and age. Work and rest. Sea and land. Anger and serenity. Faith and doubt.

Worship has this same rhythm. Christians come together as the people of God to enjoy each other as friends and neighbors, to hear the Word that stands above and that lodges in between our words, and to refill our buckets of hope. Then they *go out* to live the New Life, to bear witness to their spiritual identity and to minister to a disoriented world.

We violate our best insight whenever we seize upon either of those functions and say, "*This* is it. This is what the Christ calls upon his people to do." Mature believers do both. They know an elephant is not all trunk; a dinner is not all dessert.

If our life as a political people is to be transformed, it too must begin with a rebirth of idealism and pride, with that special energy we call "commitment."

We must sing, and sacrifice.

What we strive for is a healthy life-balance between pride and humility. Pride is one form of strength, humility another. Both also are capable of being turned into weaknesses.

Two Roman Catholic priests from different orders were having an argument. Said one, as he named several different orders, telling how one excelled by working in hospitals, another by teaching in schools, and still another by helping among the poor: "As for our order, when it comes to humility, we're tops!"

We are rubber bands, meant to expand and contract, to pray and strive. Even while we are crying in the midst of tragedy we know that out of it laughter will come again.

In Leonard Gross's book *1985—An Argument for Man,* one essay is called "Truth Is Round." Gross, who once served as West Coast editor of the now defunct *Look* magazine, traveled widely about the world and saw life at its most grim. Later he wrote:

> I've been with people whose daily meal comes from the garbage dumps of Santiago, and whose homes are built atop their source of food. I've been to an Iranian village 80 percent of whose inhabitants are blinded by trachoma. I've stood on the Nile watching women draw drinking water a few yards from a wading, urinating cow.[2]

But for every depressing sight he has found another that is heartening and hopeful, and he has come out with an optimistic book. When he says that the truth is round, what he means is that we cannot sit in front of a television set between 6:00 and 6:30 P.M. and come away with the full truth. We get a small piece of it, but what we get is the small arc of a circle.

One spring when the trees on our church grounds were in gorgeous blossom and it was raining every other day, I arrived early one morning to see the door of the music buildings plastered with wet petals. It was as if these flowers were addressing me personally and saying, Hey, have you been noticing us? Such beauty often goes far to help us win a skirmish against depression.

Rollers on the beach, wind in the pines, the slow flapping of herons across sand dunes, drown out the hectic rhythms of city and suburb, time tables and schedules. One falls under their spell, relaxes, stretches out prone. One becomes, in fact, like the element on which one lies, flattened by the sea; bare, open, empty as the beach, erased by today's tides of all yesterday's scribblings.

And then, some morning in the second week, the mind wakes, comes to life again. . . .[3]

That's Anne Morrow Lindbergh in *Gift from the Sea.*

The contradictions of goodness. The medicine of the heart. The same conviction shines forests in the Johannine prologue: "The light shines in the darkness, and the darkness has not put it out."

So we are renewed by love. We are renewed by beauty. And we are also renewed by sleep; renewed by prayer. We are even renewed by work. We are renewed by music, by a good meal and a shower, by travel. And we are renewed by laughter. We are renewed by understanding that we *are* the children of God and not the proud little masters of our own destiny. We are renewed by moonglow and by silence. And, through all of these, we are being renewed by the God who loves us and who has provided not only air for our lungs and sunlight so things can grow, but also a Savior for our humanness, our sin, and the pain of our dying and our doubts.

Jesus is our strongest link with God. In him, time and eternity come together; the human and the divine become one river, a confluence of wonder. He is both mystery and meaning for us. And, in his presence, we can never completely sell out to despair.

15. Instructions for erecting a tent in a rainstorm

> *In an age of accelerating change the past—even a glorious past—loses relevance and becomes less serviceable as a unifying principle. Typically, nations used to find their identity and unity in a heritage of blood and soil, shared by all the members, and handed down from the romantic mists of antiquity. But when traditions are attenuated by rapid change, when new knowledge gushes forth, when the identity of blood recedes to make way for individuality and diversity, when the mobility and dynamism of peoples weaken the hold of the farm and the home town, then a society will not find its unifying principle in a static idealization of a golden age that lies behind it.*
>
> Max Ways

Gatlinburg, Tennessee. That's where it happened.

It was our first night out, and first family camping experience. The Apache trailer which, when opened with a tent-top, slept four, had followed dutifully behind our car throughout the afternoon. We had stopped for a roadside cookout at five-thirty. Now, as the first signs of dusk began to appear, we were beginning to consider where we would spend the night. When you have your own bedroom with you, that isn't much of a problem. At least so we thought.

112

The pine air of the Smokies was already beginning to fill our nostrils. This was living!

First, though, we had to pass through Gatlinburg.

In spite of cautious driving, a deep dip in the street there caused the trailer hitch to break. Our minihouse went sprawling, ripping loose the wiring that lighted it at the back and causing commotion in the Saturday night traffic.

Getting out to investigate, I heard a siren. I was barely able to push the trailer to the curb before two fire trucks rushed past, grazing the seat of my pants.

Later, a Samaritan family with Mississippi license plates helped us make temporary repairs to the hitch and furnished escort service (guarding against rear-end collision) to a campground four miles out of town. Halfway there, a gulley-washing rain dropped out of the sky. What had begun as a lark in the country became a soaked sparrow looking for the dry corner of a barn.

We erected our tent in the midst of a black and wild storm.

Snuggled inside the covers about midnight, we began to laugh and sing songs.

Creative moments are nearly always unserene.

Like childbirth.

1776.

Or sharp moments of sorrow, when love and memory gleam with the luminosity of August stars. Moments when life and death fuse into a single truth.

What we are looking for today is not tranquility, but direction. Twenty years ago our national identity was neatly rooted in the past. Today it is anchored in mid-air. Openness of life and an expectant attitude concerning the future may be able to furnish what the past cannot. Our times seem to call for *tent*-ative rather than final value structures in faith as well as politics—a willingness to live under canvas.

113

Geophysicists are positive now about a phenomenon called "continental motion." Though the rate at which continents move seems incredibly slow—six or seven inches a year—to those who measure time in eons, the pace is breathtaking. Fifty million years from now North America and Europe will be seven hundred miles further apart. The Panama Canal will no longer be needed. Central America will have broken away from South America. Los Angeles will slide underneath the Aleutian Islands.

This is true of life. Life, as we have already contended, sings and it swings. It moves and vibrates. It is a river, not a mountain. It is as exciting, as turbulent as time. And a storm is beautiful if you think it is.

Dying to coldness is part of the chemistry of love. Death is not losing; it is being caught up with action. It is the mystery of that exchange without which God's dream would stagnate and stop.

And poise—

Nothing useful was ever accomplished in panic. We cannot make sound decisions if we're rattled or supertired. But some things can't wait.

An unmarried girl finds she is pregnant, and knows she must adopt a strategy.

Election day arrives: a box has to be checked.

Sixty-fifth birthdays: mandatory retirement. But faith, in at least one of its forms, is coolness—that quality of spirit which generates endurance.

A suggestion I sometimes pass along to persons who find themselves in trouble is one by Robert Spike, a young minister who was grotesquely murdered on the Ohio State University campus in the late 1960s. Among his personal papers were these sentences:

114

If one were to pick out a virtue for the Christian life, endurance would be a good one. To stand in the face of the storm, with courage and without panic, is perhaps a more needed ingredient of Christian love than sympathy. This is not an endurance appropriate to the Stoic. It is cold and gray, built of despair. It is endurance that is warmed by the mysterious love of God, even in the worst of human situations. More than that, this evidence is taken as a token of a final crazy hope that God shall fully reign over his creation.

Man has been around for 50,000 years, and this divides up into approximately 800 lifetimes. There's nothing shocking about that. But he does make us blink when he says that our lifetime is splitting history into two qualitatively different parts.

The first 650 were spent in caves. Only during the last 70 lifetimes has it been possible to communicate effectively from one lifetime to another. Only during the last four has it been possible to measure time with precision, and only in the last two has anyone anywhere used an electric motor. Now, within one lifetime, the original platform of civilization, agriculture, has lost its dominance and been replaced in nation after nation by industrialism.

Within one lifetime, man's top speed has gone from a maximum of 100 mph in 1880 to 17,000 mph in 1963. His ascent above the earth from 60,000 feet, when I was in high school, to 250,000 miles in 1969.

For 799 of these lifetimes, change was slow, evolutionary, and gradual. But in the middle of the twentieth century, history exploded, giving us the chance to live many lifetimes in one. The old options remain: the choice between life and death. But now they have been raised to the 800th power.

115

In a society where transience rather than permanence is stenciled onto everything we touch—as old worlds die and new ones emerge—we need to learn the art of graceful death.

An operatic coach offered to teach students "how to die without hurting yourself." That may be the art we must learn if our humanity is to succeed: to let the past go without mourning so that the future can arrive with rejoicing.

Strangely, death teaches us about life more than life teaches us about death. Above everything else, Christians are supposed to know how to die, and our awakening each morning is another anniversary of resurrection. Yet we often wear the pallor of those for whom the splendor of living seems to have vanished.

In life we are in the midst of death.

Carlyle Marney tells how, on returning from summer vacations in the woods, his children would call back, as the family automobile pulled away from the mountain retreat, where they had spent happy days: "Good-by, little house; good-by, trees!"

Every good-by is death. And some "deaths" come in the giant size: moral systems, religions, civilizations, galaxies, God.

The "good deaths," though, are those of the emotions that undercut our joy and our role as positive people.

Like fear. We are born with fear. And our fear grows the more we learn about evil. We begin with the fear of falling, darkness, the unknown. Later there is the fear of not being accepted. Still later, the fear that goes along with facing up to the possibility that life has no meaning, that God is a fiction invented to counteract the cold sweat that rolls off him when he comes to know that nothing endures.

We cannot be free until we die to the tyranny of fear.

Fear depletes us; makes us tense, unhappy, vulnerable;

116

cuts us off from people around us, forces us into bad decisions, and keeps us from sleeping and laughing. Fear of disapproval converts us into cowards. Fear violates the gift of life.

Another "good" death involves conceit. We can become our own biggest problem if we are without anything to lift us up out of ourselves. In dealing with grief, one thing helps more than anything: getting about and getting involved with the grief of others, discovering we have not been singled out for injury.

Charley was past ninety, and he hardly ever missed worship. One Sunday morning after I had preached with great seriousness and intensity, I stood at the rear door greeting the people, and Charlie came by. He grasped my hand in a loving way, looked me directly in the eye, and, with a twinkle, said: "Smile!"

A priest I know was talking about how hard it is to please the congregation. He said: "I often feel that with just a little bit more effort, I could displease everybody! This week is quite typical. My associate preached on Sunday. In Monday's mail, I received a long letter signed by a number of the parish. The first paragraph said, 'We had begun to suspect that communism had infiltrated the Roman Catholic Church, and now after the associate's sermon yesterday, we know it.' "

He said the first paragraph didn't bother him so much. He was glad to have the congregation working over the associate for awhile instead of him. But the second paragraph did get to him. It said, "What was worse than the associate's sermon, Father, was that you sat up there nodding your head in approval."

"Dare I tell them," he said, "that I wasn't nodding my head in approval at all? I was just nodding."

Preachers and churches also sometimes come up for review

117

in beauty shops. One woman recently shouted above the noise of the dryer to the person beside her that she had developed the suspicion that her minister no longer believed in God. She asked whether this neighbor was faring any better where she attended.

To believe in God is a tougher task than saying a quick yes to the Apostles' Creed. If anyone tells me he finds it easy to believe in God, I find him hard to believe. Ours is a radical time. Our thoughts about God are half-old, half-new. But this isn't God's first experience at cross-examination.

He is greater than our questions, more faithful than our faith, more loving than our love.

That's as good news as I can bring.

16. Yes got up before the sun

> In the resurrection something or someone is
> saying to me, "Don't worry if your nerve ends
> tremble at the very thought of pain and death;
> that is what I made nerves for. But I transcend
> nerves. I invented them. I can annul their
> messages. Don't worry about trying to imagine
> literally what plans I have for you. The nymph
> or the dragonfly crawling on the bottom of the
> lake cannot know, except through poetic
> rumors, the meaning of sunlight, the ocean of air,
> glistening wings, green leaves. My story of an
> empty tomb shows what I am and what you
> shall be. Sing the story until you and the story
> and the music are one. Translate the story
> into any new mythological language that your
> voice can sing. Sing. Live one day at a time.
> Leave the rest to me. Sing!"

> Chad Walsh

Easter is the brightest, most elegant day in the Christian year. All it lacks is fireworks. It is a day for flowers, pretty clothes, egg hunts, feasting, and music that shakes the rafters of a thousand churches.

It ends the Lenten dark.

It turns Good Friday inside out.

Its mood is victory, like Election Eve, when the returns are coming in and they're in our favor.

Its theme is life.

119

Its favorite word is "Alleluia!"

It's the day Yes got up before the sun.

Still, when a minister tries to level with his people as to what Easter means, and what the celebration is all about, he knows he must talk with them about death. Death and life are somehow so interrelated we cannot understand one without talking about the other.

Rollo May has written: "I wonder if we could love passionately, if ecstasy would be possible at all if we knew we'd never die."

If Christ is risen, and I believe he is, that is information and a reality that applies to the next twenty-four hours, not merely to some futuristic speculation concerning a Beautiful Isle of Somewhere. The Church is not an insurance company; it is a laboratory which holds life up to the sunlight, that asks important questions each week about what it means and what its priorities ought to be.

The Easter life is on the line for us daily.

If Christ is risen, and I believe he is, then the Resurrection is something we already participate in, because we are an Easter people. Freed from the horror which overtakes our mental world when we think of death apart from faith, we are set free to laugh and live, relax and serve—to drink deeply of the cup of life fifty-two weeks a year.

Is there life after death? Is there a way to be sure? How can the heart really know?

When Christian, of *Pilgrim's Progress,* came within sight of the eternal city, he tried to look at it through his glass but his hands shook so he could not clearly see.

Paul, whose words make up more than half of the New Testament, wrote, "Eye has not seen, nor ear heard, neither has entered into the understanding of man the wonderful things God has prepared for those who love him."

The stage production *Jesus Christ, Superstar* omitted the

Resurrection altogether. In its place was substituted the unresolved suggestion of a section of violins. In the celluloid version the Resurrection is expressed by an empty seat on a bus.

One way of looking at the Resurrection might add up to this: we are dealing with something that is totally beyond us, so why talk about it? Plainly, we do not know. From that remote country no traveler has ever returned. The nitty-gritty of life after death turns out to be not a hard-hitting communiqué from the front. Instead, it winds up as the same old guessing game, combined with the same old hard-to-believe stories about an empty tomb, a group of men walking along a rural road in the direction of Emmaus, and trembling Thomas reaching out to touch nail holes in the hands of a crucified friend.

It's the essence of the faith adventure, and faith can never be less than an adventure. Faith is not a sure thing. It's a thrust into the darkness but a thrust we make with the name of Jesus upon our lips.

The Resurrection is more of a mirror than an historical truth. It is a mirror in which we see reflections of our own Royal destiny.

The Jesus of history is a mirror in which we see the human face of God.

The cross is another mirror in which we see that God conquers through weakness, suffering, and sacrifice more convincingly than he does through power and force.

And his presence as the Risen Lord, manifested to and among his followers, even after he had been killed, is a third mirror in which we see the most overwhelming truth of all: death is not the final fact in the universe. Life wins!

Are we to be satisfied with these broad, optimistic, life-affirming principles? Is that as far as confirmation goes?

I remember a question once asked me by a family who had

lost a son on a battlefield. I spoke of the Christian hope. I quoted Jesus' statement to the disciples "I will see you again" and words like "If these houses of ours are destroyed, we have a building of God, a house not made with hands, eternal in the heavens" (2 Cor. 5:1). I repeated a story of Peter Marshall's about how death might be likened to a playing youngster who falls asleep on the floor with his clothes on and awakens the next morning to find himself in his own bed in his pajamas, rested, and with the light of a new morning pouring through the windows, offering the prospect of another day of play and fun. I put my arms around the father's shoulder. I prayed with the family and tried to lift them out of their darkness: and they were grateful for these acts of comfort and sympathy. But the father could not resist asking the question of questions: "I still want to know," he said, "what happened to that boy."

It's too late to answer the father now. I guess we could say his inquiry has become moot, for he has since joined his son in the land we're talking about. But his question still rocks the atmosphere and the hearts of an infinite number of other families and persons. It still leaps embarrassingly upward for some answer.

Christian faith makes this reply: the love of God is big enough and strong enough and true enough to cope with the matter of this boy's dying. If death were stronger than life, or beyond God's power to do anything about, God would not be God. This is God's world, and we are the inventions of his heart. Our imaginations are not agile enough to conceive where this boy is today, or what he is doing, or what goes on in heaven, or what new expressions his new life takes. What we do know is that he has not disappeared forever, leaving only a warm glow of memory or beneficent influence behind. The statement in the Creed "I believe in the Resurrection of the body"—or as I wish it read, "the Resurrection of the person"—renounces that.

The Christian faith believes there is an ultimate and loving meaning which lies at the heart of things.

This does not mean everything in the world makes sense. It does not.

Each year hundreds of children die of cancer. That does not make sense. It does not add up to anything resembling a wisely planned or beautifully ordered universe. But beyond our restricted vision and understanding, our perplexity—our sometimes bitter anger—there is a Voice which says: life is not absurd! Even the tears of the race with which the earth is soaked from crust to center cannot cancel out for us the ecstatic, bittersweet conviction that life, with all of its incongruities, is magnificent material. That sacramental meaning, even if only partly understood, hovers around us all the time.

So we can deny—at least, I think we can—that the world always makes the kind of sense we think it should, if God is any kind of gentleman at all. We can deny it and still hold to the inward music, to an irreducible and indestructible certainty that the world *does* make Final Sense—that it is *that* kind of world—that we belong to God: to God's love, and to God's plans, and not to hell or simply silence.

Dr. Harry Emerson Fosdick once asked: "Is this a world that saves its lowest, clinging to dust with tenacious eagerness, and with careless fingers throws spirit all away?"

He puts his answer in the form of a parable:

Suppose you had a magnificent house, and suppose that through the halls and up the stairs and around the galleries of that house there played a child, your child, and suppose that some day fire threatened and you had to choose which you would keep, your house and lose the

123

child, we should know you to be as insane as you are wicked, as wicked as you are insane. Is this an insane universe that keeps the house and lets the children go, that clings to matter and cares not for spirit, that hugs dust and throws the soul away. . . ? [1]

As Professor Palmer of Harvard said about his wife's death, who can fail to feel the irrationality of the universe "if out of deference to a few particles of disordered matter it excludes so fair a spirit? Thank God for the Easter message, affirming that God's world is not thus mad, but that while the physical passes, the spiritual endures!"

Easter comes down to this: what kind of explanation of the universe will we be satisfied with? If the earth is only a complex machine, then what I have written in this book, and what the New Testament hopes to help us see, is sentimental slop, a copout that can't face the stern truth of a man's dying.

But I can no more accept that—intellectually, emotionally, or religiously—than I can accept the fact that that's what a man is: a bunch of circuits, a crazy combination of plumbing, levers, miniaturized cameras, and hair-covered textile.

Man is God's love-child, endowed with divine spirit, so precious no words could come anywhere near defining his significance. I know that is true, not because I know myself, but because I have loved, and have seen that wonder, that light, that ultimacy of value in my children, my wife, my parents, and in others who, for me, have validated the Christian expectancy and trust beyond any of the claims of formal theology.

On a flight from Rome to London, we flew one morning over the Alps shortly after a storm had covered them with a fresh snowfall. It was a magical feeling—snugly flying five or six hundred miles an hour four miles high over that white fairyland in a sleek and powerful aircraft, the pilot thoughtfully tipping the wings from side to side so people on either side of the plane might get a view of the sight below.

The aerodynamic lift of those wings was invisible to the human eye, but how real, how fantastically strong it was! You can't see an idea, either. And you can't see the gravitational energies by which the stars are organized, according to whose same invisible authority the galaxies turn. You can't see the spirit of man any more than you can see the spirit of God. You can't see love. Or hope. Or faith. Yet nothing is any more real, or quite as enduring as all of these.

The Easter world is a big world. Not a cramped world. Not a dying world, but a world in which life is being constantly exchanged for other life.

Those Alps below, with their strong snowy shoulders! They seem dead, but if we could go down and explore beneath the snow we might find the life of a million blue forget-me-nots waiting for those warm signals of the sun that will soon cause them to laugh and bloom again along the rough, gray edges of those glacial humps.

One of those tiny perishable flowers is more marvelous than all the Alps. The mountains stand static for centuries but the flower grows. It dies, but is reborn from its own seeds which it creates.

So don't underestimate the Miracle, or underbelieve it. Don't shrink the world down to your size. That's idolatry. That's dressing up and playing God, putting yourself in the center—not the larger love you were born to worship and adore.

When I was thirteen, I had my first real taste of death. Tiny, my fox-terrier, was struck by a car and killed. I discovered the stiff white form by the side of a graveled road one evening near sunset. After I had broken the news at

125

home, it was decided to leave the dog in a vacant lot nearby, under a cover, until morning. Then, according to my Dad, we could give him a proper burial.

The next morning I arose at four-thirty to carry the *Des Moines Register*. It was raining. When I finished the route about six, light was starting to break. The rain, though, was still coming down hard.

Soaked from the downpour, I made my way over to the vacant lot to mourn. Standing alone there in the half-darkness, sobbing with grief, I did not hear my father's approach from behind. Suddenly, though, I became aware of him, standing so close his coarse blue Big Smith overalls gently touched me to form a partial shelter from the weather.

He said not a word. But a glorious comfort rolled over me in that moment.

Since then it has always been easy to call God my Father.

A good friend, Arthur Sueltz, says it well—in words that have especially happy connotations for every home where children run and weep and struggle with homework and get tucked into bed at night:

> When my children were small I used to throw them up in the air, or sometimes take them in my arms and spin them down on the bed. And after I'd done that half a dozen times, usually with bright shining eyes they'd look up and say, "Do it again, Daddy, do it again." Studdert-Kennedy thought he could see the whole world of men and women standing before their great Father, as their strength began to fail, but with their eyes still shining and say, "Do it again, Daddy, do it again." As though we always try to recapture the ecstasy of life. But can never quite get hold of it. Here we stand in a world of dying things and dying people, but still able to say, "Do it again, Daddy, do it again." And we keep

saying it until that moment he reaches down and picks us up and holds us to his heart forever. Our Father keeps the best wine until the last. And he gives me Easter to let me know that in the midst of death I am in life everlasting.[2]

The Resurrection is not a Houdini trick, it's a sign—the other half of the Bethlehem star. Not a hearts and flowers routine we go through once a year to cheer ourselves up, but rather the authentic data of who we are and of Life that cannot be destroyed regardless of the collapse of our physical bodies. Easter is promise and Easter is Yes! Choice: we must choose whether to believe the Star and Sign, or cry ourselves to sleep; to split the sky with our praise, or waste our strength in resentment and fear. We must choose between suicide or adoration—and we do!

Easter is life's most striking Yes, as new as this very morning's sunlight, as personal as your fingerprints or mine.

Easter is people and Easter is hope.

Easter is God, incarnate in the plain bread of ordinary life. Is anything ordinary? A child's mouth, a mother's hands, a river running through the woods?

Easter is kissing and snuggling in bed, picnics, and going to work on Monday morning. It's memories and twilight talk. It's taking a large, deep breath, purging away the smallest trace of anxious fear.

Two people trusting each other—faith's permanent rebuttal to despair.

A pair of wings to fly with.

A thunderous explosion, and, in the same instant, a miracle as soundless as a sailboat, visible on a blue-edged horizon—a found horizon, not a lost one.

Easter is laughter.

Easter is life.

Easter is Yes.

And Yes is a World, the truest World of all.

It belongs to you, and to me, but we have to establish our claim. That's what makes each day so deliciously worth living.

Notes

Chapter 1

Headnote: Wallace Stevens, from "Credences of Summer," in *The Collected Poems of Wallace Stevens* (New York: Alfred A. Knopf, 1969), p. 373. Used by permission.
1. e. e. cummings, *Collected Poems 1913–1962* (New York: Harcourt Brace Jovanich, Inc.), no. 271 from section entitled "No Thanks." Used by permission.
2. James Joyce, *Ulysses* (New York: Random House, Modern Library, new ed. corrected and reset, 1961), p. 783.
3. Norman Corwin, "Prayer for the Seventies," in the *Journal of the Screen Producers Guild of America*. Copyright 1969 by Norman Corwin.
4. Robert Raines, from "Easter in Our Eyes," in *Lord, Could You Make It a Little Better?* (Waco, Texas: Word Books, 1972), p. 144.

Chapter 2

Headnote: Roderic Gorney, M.D., *The Human Agenda* (New York: Simon & Schuster, 1968), p. 572. Used by permission.
1. Carl Sandburg, from "The People, Yes," in *Complete Poems* (New York: Harcourt Brace Jovanich, Inc., 1950), p. 568.
2. James W. Angell, "The Whole World Is Munich."
3. René Dubos, *A God Within* (New York: Charles Scribner's Sons, 1972), pp. 293–94.

Chapter 3

Headnote: Quoted from an interview in the *Los Angeles Times* with book editor Digby Diehl. Used by permission of Digby Diehl.
1. Judith Schwab, "Man at the Counter," copyright 1971 Christian Century Foundation. Reprinted by permission from the April 28, 1971, issue of *The Christian Century*.

Yes is a world

Chapter 4

Headnote: Alfred North Whitehead, *Process and Reality*, p. 526. Copyright 1929 by Macmillan Publishing Co., Inc., renewed by Evelyn Whitehead. Used by permission.
1. Rainer Maria Rilke, *Letters to a Young Poet* (New York: Norton, 1954).
2. Used by permission of Mr. and Mrs. Hal Boyd of Santa Monica, California.

Chapter 6

Headnote: Chaim Potok, *The Chosen* (Greenwich, Conn.: Fawcett Publications, 1967), p. 249. Used by permission of Simon & Schuster.
1. Grace Hazard Conkling, "After Sunset," in *Masterpieces of Religious Verse*, ed. James Dalton Morrison (New York: Harper & Row, 1948), p. 589. Reprinted by permission of Harper & Row, Publishers.
2. Ralph Spaulding Cushman, "The Secret," in *Masterpieces of Religious Verse*, p. 589.
3. George M. Docherty, "The Silences of God," *One Way of Living* (New York: Harper & Row, 1958), p. 111.
4. Kenneth Jones, personal statement from a church bulletin of Lakewood Presbyterian Church, San Francisco. Used by permission.

Chapter 7

1. George Buttrick, *The Parables of Jesus* (New York: Harper & Row, 1928), p. 75.

Chapter 8

1. R. Lofton Hudson, *Persons in Crisis* (Nashville, Tenn.: Broadman Press, 1969), p. 120. Used by permission.
2. R. Lofton Hudson, ibid., p. 111. Used by permission.

Notes

Chapter 9

Headnote: James W. Angell, "Cameo Appearance."
1. Chaim Potok, *The Chosen* (Greenwich, Conn.: Fawcett Publications, 1967). Used by permission of Simon & Schuster, Inc.

Chapter 10

Headnote: Excerpt from "*Playboy* Interview: Ingmar Bergman," *Playboy* Magazine; copyright © 1964 by Cynthia Grenier.
1. Helen Keller, *The Story of My Life* (Garden City, N.Y.: Doubleday, Doran & Co., 1941), pp. 29–31.
2. Lois Wyse, "Lines to an Unhandy Man," in *Love Poems for the Very Married* (New York: World, 1967), p. 45.
3. e. e. cummings, *Collected Poems 1913–1962* (New York: Harcourt Brace Jovanich, Inc.), no. 271 from section entitled "No Thanks." Used by permission.

Chapter 11

Headnote: Used by permission of Dr. William M. MacInnes, San Diego, California, a personal friend of the author.
1. George Romanes, cited by Dr. Viktor E. Frankl in *Man's Search for Meaning* (New York: Washington Square Press, 1963), pp. 188–90.
2. Ibid.

Chapter 12

1. Dr. Page Smith, "Flight from the Home," *San Francisco Chronicle*, June 13, 1973, p. 40. Copyright, Los Angeles Times. Reprinted with permission of Times Post/News Service.

Chapter 13

Headnote: From Harvey Cox's *Feast of Fools* (Cambridge, Mass.: Harvard University Press, 1969), p. 55.
1. William James, *Pragmatism and Other Essays* (New York:

Washington Square Press, 1963), pp. 283–84. Used by permission of Simon & Schuster, Inc.
2. Harry Emerson Fosdick, *Riverside Sermons* (New York: Harper & Row, 1958), p. 325.
3. Harvey Cox, *Feast of Fools*, p. 55.

Chapter 14

Headnote: David Redding, poem from *Until You Bless Me* (Grand Rapids, Mich.: Wm. B. Eerdmans, 1972). Used by permission.
1. William Wordsworth, *The World Is Too Much With Us*, Ib, xxxiiv.
2. Leonard Gross, "Truth Is Round," in *1985: An Argument for Man* (New York: W. W. Norton, Inc., 1971), p. 25. Used by permission.
3. Anne Morrow Lindbergh, *Gift from the Sea* (New York: Pantheon Books, 1955), p. 16.

Chapter 15

Headnote: Max Ways, "Finding the American Direction." Reprinted from the October 1970 issue of *Fortune* Magazine by special permission; © 1970 TIME, Inc.

Chapter 16

Headnote: Chad Walsh, *God at Large* (New York: Seabury Press, 1971), p. 126. Used by permission.
1. Harry Emerson Fosdick, *Riverside Sermons*, p. 126.
2. By permission of Arthur Sueltz, minister of Lakewood Presbyterian Church, Long Beach, California.

To
Helen and Dana Card
of
Lexington, Kentucky,
whose quiet witness to so many
of the good things of life makes
me want to be worthy of our
friendship